Toddlercare

JUNE THOMPSON RGN, RM, RHV

CARROLL & BROWN PUBLISHERS LIMITED

This edition first published
in the United Kingdom in 2002 by
Carroll & Brown Publishers Limited
20 Lonsdale Road
London NW6 6RD

A CIP record for this book is available from the British Library
ISBN 1-903258-36-7

First published with spiral binding in the United Kingdom
in 1997 by HarperCollins Publishers

CONTENTS

FOREWORD

*A*s a health visitor, I was delighted to be asked to write a book devoted solely to the care of toddlers. For many years I have been conscious that there is often a gap between the help and information available to parents of a new baby, and that for parents of toddlers. During the first year of a baby's life, parents usually have access to a wealth of information. They are encouraged to attend a child health clinic and health professionals readily give advice on common problems.

As their baby grows and they gain experience, parents acquire more confidence and competence. But when their baby becomes a toddler, new problems and concerns often arise. A happy compliant baby may alter almost overnight into a whinging, disobedient toddler. Worries may arise over developmental progress, such as walking or talking. Public attitudes towards babies and toddlers may also change. Admiring glances given to a sleeping baby can turn to disapproving frowns for the active toddler tearing up the supermarket aisle; and sympathy for the mother of the child having a temper tantrum is usually less than that for a crying baby. Other people's children often seem to behave better than their own, parents may blame themselves for any perceived shortcomings in their child, and confidence in their parenting skills may therefore falter further.

Getting help with caring for toddlers is not, however, always easy. Baby books may not provide enough in-depth information on toddlers and specialist books may only cover specific problems. Parents who regularly used a child health clinic with a young baby sometimes feel out of place with a toddler. A busy health professional may not always have sufficient time to answer a parent's concerns fully. In this book, I have tried to cover all aspects of a toddler's development, and answer the types of questions that parents have asked me over many years. But apart from giving plenty of love, there is no perfect or correct way to bring up a child. Each one is unique and requires an individual approach. More importantly, because bringing up a toddler should be enjoyable, lots of fun activities and suggestions of things to do with your toddler are included. I hope you find it useful.

I would like to thank the staff of Carroll & Brown for their assistance and expertise in producing this book, Amy Carroll for her ideas about the contents and additions, Sharon Freed for her excellent editing, and the design and production staff.

DAILY ROUTINES

It is important to establish a routine that suits both you and your toddler, in all aspects of your child's everyday care. Remember that your child is an individual, so be prepared to be flexible. Bear in mind too that the habits your child learns at this stage will be carried on into later life, affecting his health, personal hygiene, sleeping and eating patterns.

MEETING YOUR TODDLER'S NUTRITIONAL NEEDS

Good nutrition combined with healthy eating habits developed during the toddler years will lay the building blocks for future good health. A balanced diet ensures that your child's nutritional needs for energy and growth are met. A good diet also helps to protect your child against illness and infection, and aids his mental development and ability to learn.

A healthy diet for toddlers is not necessarily the same as that for adults. Toddlers have very high daily requirements for energy (calories) and other nutrients – this is particularly true after they begin to walk as they become more active and grow quickly. Because their stomachs are small, however, toddlers cannot eat large amounts of food at one sitting – a toddler-sized serving is usually a third to a half of an adult's. They therefore need three main meals a day with nourishing snacks in-between. They need to eat easily digestible and nutrient-rich foods from the five food groups shown below.

THE FIVE MAIN FOOD GROUPS
If your child regularly eats something from each of the main food groups, then he is likely to get all the nutrients (protein, carbohydrate, fat, vitamins and minerals) he requires for good health.

Fat and sugar
A balanced diet should provide sufficient amounts of these. Refined sugars should be avoided. Use full-fat dairy products.

Meat and meat alternatives
Aim for one meat, fish or egg serving daily, or two from plant sources such as pulses or beans.

Dairy products
Aim for at least 350 ml (½ pint) full-fat milk daily or two servings of cheese, fromage frais or yoghurt.

Fruit and vegetables
Aim for at least four servings daily of fresh, tinned or frozen fruit and vegetables. Fruit juice should count as only one serving even if given more than once.

Grain products and starchy foods
Aim for at least one serving each mealtime of bread, corn, rice, cereal or starchy vegetables. Avoid very rough grains.

HOW MUCH FIBRE?

Some fibre is necessary in your child's diet to prevent constipation, but too much may fill him up so that he does not want other foods. A high-fibre diet may also lead to diarrhoea and can interfere with absorption of minerals such as iron.

If your child eats a variety of grains and fruits and vegetables daily, or a combination of white and wholemeal varieties of bread and breakfast cereals, he is likely to be getting enough fibre.

SHOULD HE EAT FATS?

Fat is a concentrated source of energy and vitamins for young children and also provides essential fatty acids. It is best that your child obtain most of his fat from foods such as whole milk, or cheese, which also contain other essential nutrients. Foods such as crisps and biscuits may be high in fat but are usually poor in other nutrients, so these should be limited. Meat should be lean.

Skimmed or low-fat milk should not be given to children under the age of five. Semi-skimmed milk may be given from the age of two if you are sure that your child is getting enough energy (calories) from a good mixed diet. If in doubt ask your doctor or health visitor for advice.

VITAMIN SUPPLEMENTS

Your toddler may need A, C and D supplements if his diet is not rich in foods containing these

A VARIED DIET
Allowing your child to help you prepare food may encourage her to eat more healthily.

nutrients. However, you should always check with your doctor on the recommended dose of supplements as too much of these vitamins can be just as dangerous as too little.

ZINC AND IRON REQUIREMENTS

An iron deficiency can slow down your toddler's growth and development. Try to give your child some foods containing iron every day. To increase iron absorption give some food or fruit juice containing vitamin C at every meal.

Good sources of iron include red meat, oily fish (such as canned sardines and pilchards), shellfish, fortified breakfast cereals, bread, eggs, dried fruits (such as raisins, apricots, and dates), beans and pulses (such as canned baked beans, pinto beans, chick peas and lentils), oranges, apricots, green peas and dark leafy greens (such as cabbage and broccoli).

Zinc is necessary for a healthy immune system and for growth. Good sources include meat and poultry, wholegrain cereals, zinc-fortified cereals, hard cheese, eggs, pulses and beans.

Avoid giving your toddler tannin-containing foods or drinks such as tea with his meals as tannin inhibits the absorption of iron and zinc.

SAFETY FIRST WITH FOODS

Avoid giving these foods to toddlers:

▶ Any nuts (especially peanuts), popcorn, and fruit with stones or pips, because of the risk of choking.

▶ Caffeine-containing foods or beverages as caffeine may make your toddler irritable.

▶ Highly spiced food unless your child is used to it and asks for it.

▶ Excessively salty dishes as these will make him very thirsty.

EATING WITH THE FAMILY

Learning to eat with the rest of the family is an important part of your child's social development. If you normally have your evening meal late, and your toddler has already eaten, you could still let her sit with you and give her some finger foods on which to nibble. Also, try to have breakfast with your child, or to eat together at weekends.

At mealtimes, much more than food is going into your child – she is learning social skills such as how to use eating utensils, to communicate and to share and enjoy food. So it is important to make these relaxed and happy occasions. Otherwise, sitting down and eating at a table can be boring to a child or can turn into a battle of wills between parents and child. Bear in mind too that children copy adults – if you eat your food with enjoyment, your child is more likely to do so as well. If she gets bored at the table, let her get down from her chair and play on the floor.

Be realistic about what to expect from your toddler. Some mess is inevitable when she is learning to feed herself. Cover her with a large bib and put some newspaper or plastic covering on the floor. By the time she is 15–18 months old she should be able to bring food to her mouth

HIGH CHAIRS

When buying a high chair make sure it is sturdy and has both a waist and a crotch strap. It should be secure enough to stop your child standing up in it. Also, the tray should be large to give support for her arms and have raised edges to catch spills, and should be removable for easy washing.

You may prefer to get a feeding table which is lower and more stable than a high chair but it will take up more room and is not as practical if the toddler is eating at the family table.

with a spoon without too many spills, although finger feeding may be quicker. She may also want you to feed her sometimes if she is tired.

Don't worry too much about table manners at this age, but set limits of what you find unacceptable, such as food being thrown on the floor or at someone.

By three years of age your toddler should be able to handle a fork and spoon with some dexterity but will need help with a knife, particularly in cutting up large pieces of food. Build in more time than you think you need for mealtimes as your child learns to feed herself – and applaud her efforts. Always give small servings; give seconds if she asks. Don't offer bribes for her to finish her meal or reward her if she does.

Once your child is old enough, let her help you to prepare food such as putting her own spread on bread or a topping on pizza, and let her help you to lay the table.

EATING OUT

If you are going out for the day take plenty of snack foods such as fruits, sandwiches, pieces of cheese and fruit juices, as toddlers get irritable if they don't eat for a long time. Carry wet wipes or cloths to wipe her hands before eating and her mouth afterwards.

SELF-FEEDING
Learning to feed herself with a spoon is an important part of a toddler's physical development.

It is also a good idea to take your child to a café or restaurant occasionally as this will teach her to eat in company and to be sociable. It also provides an opportunity to eat new foods.

Some places, however, may be ill-equipped for toddlers and young children which may make the experience stressful for you and no fun for your toddler. So make sure you try to choose a restaurant that is 'family-friendly' and provides high chairs, and always order foods that are quick to prepare.

MENU IDEAS
Once your child is about a year old she can eat most of the same foods as the rest of the family, mashed or chopped as necessary and of course in smaller portions.

Remember, if your child is eating some foods from each of the main food groups (see page 6) on a daily basis, or even over several days, she is having a varied diet.

The following toddler meals combine foods from two or more of the food groups, and are healthy and simple to prepare. Bear in mind that your toddler may like to choose food for herself so offer her choices from a range of foods. Around the age of five you can gradually start the transition to the lower-fat, more adult type of diet.

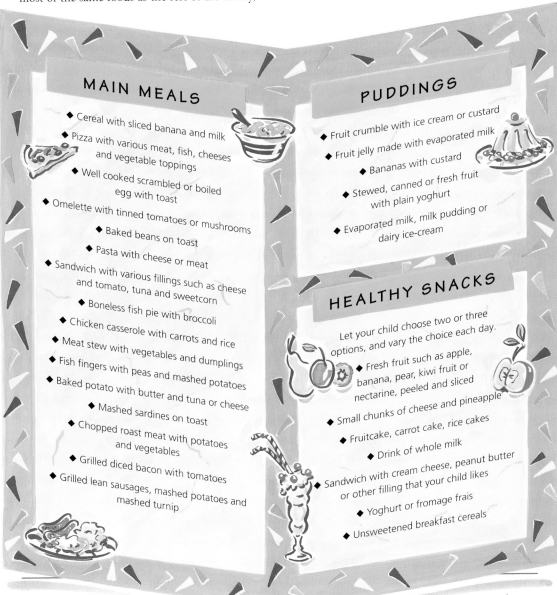

MAIN MEALS

- Cereal with sliced banana and milk
- Pizza with various meat, fish, cheeses and vegetable toppings
- Well cooked scrambled or boiled egg with toast
- Omelette with tinned tomatoes or mushrooms
- Baked beans on toast
- Pasta with cheese or meat
- Sandwich with various fillings such as cheese and tomato, tuna and sweetcorn
- Boneless fish pie with broccoli
- Chicken casserole with carrots and rice
- Meat stew with vegetables and dumplings
- Fish fingers with peas and mashed potatoes
- Baked potato with butter and tuna or cheese
- Mashed sardines on toast
- Chopped roast meat with potatoes and vegetables
- Grilled diced bacon with tomatoes
- Grilled lean sausages, mashed potatoes and mashed turnip

PUDDINGS

- Fruit crumble with ice cream or custard
- Fruit jelly made with evaporated milk
- Bananas with custard
- Stewed, canned or fresh fruit with plain yoghurt
- Evaporated milk, milk pudding or dairy ice-cream

HEALTHY SNACKS

Let your child choose two or three options, and vary the choice each day.

- Fresh fruit such as apple, banana, pear, kiwi fruit or nectarine, peeled and sliced
- Small chunks of cheese and pineapple
- Fruitcake, carrot cake, rice cakes
- Drink of whole milk
- Sandwich with cream cheese, peanut butter or other filling that your child likes
- Yoghurt or fromage frais
- Unsweetened breakfast cereals

Feeding problems

Many toddlers go through a faddy stage of eating and may refuse to eat a number of kinds of foods or will choose the same foods day after day. Your child also may have such a small appetite that you worry he is under-nourished. Fortunately, all foods provide some nutrients, and no one food is essential to health. Neither will a normal child voluntarily starve himself.

Most feeding problems resolve themselves with time and if your child is growing, is gaining weight and has plenty of energy then he is unlikely to be nutritionally deficient. If you are worried that your child is under- or overweight, ask your health visitor or doctor to check his weight for his height and age. Also, if food refusal is combined with any symptoms of illness, such as tiredness or fever, seek medical advice.

FUSSY EATERS

Toddlers not only routinely refuse certain foods and enjoy others to excess, but they often develop a taste for rituals – for example, they will only eat sandwiches that are cut in triangles.

★ Try to humour your toddler's whims as far as possible, but when he is being unreasonably disruptive, be firm but calm. Getting annoyed about your child's refusal to eat something will usually make the matter worse and it can become a power struggle between you. As he develops he will want to exert his independence, and refusing food is

one way he is able to do this. Like adults, your child cannot be expected to eat everything. Think of your toddler as an individual with his own eating habits and appetite.

A refusal to eat at mealtimes, however, can be the result of too many snacks or liquids or filling up with junk food during the day.

★ Offer a variety of foods to your child. If he refuses to eat one type of food then substitute another from the same food group. Milk, for example, can be incorporated into puddings or used on cereals, or other dairy products such as cheese can be substituted. Fruit can be puréed with milk, and vegetables added to casseroles.

★ When introducing a new food, do it when you know your child is hungry and more likely to take it. Serve brightly coloured foods and make them fun – perhaps arranging them in a pattern or let him make a pattern.

★ Don't try to bribe your child to eat a food he dislikes with foods he likes – it may make him refuse all foods. Above all, be honest about your own eating habits. If you are a fussy eater yourself, your child will pick this up and copy you.

A PREFERENCE FOR JUNK FOOD

Obesity and tooth decay will affect the occasional toddler. The cause is usually a diet high in fat, sugar and other refined carbohydrates. While there is no need to completely avoid giving your child foods such as crisps, cakes, chocolates and sweets, you should limit these to special occasions or certain days of the week (e.g. Saturday and Sunday). Don't let your child fill up on them or eat them as a substitute for a meal.

Instead of sweetened drinks or soda, give your child water or diluted unsweetened fruit juice.

THE FUSSY EATER
Offering your toddler a popular food choice at a time when he is hungry and not distracted is the best way of ensuring he will eat.

THE MESSY EATER
Rather than trying to prevent your toddler making a mess, take precautions, such as a plastic sheet under the chair, to minimise your cleaning up afterwards.

This is better for his overall health, his teeth and discourages the development of a 'sweet tooth'.

MESSY EATERS

For some children, food is an adventure and they prefer to do everything with it except eat it. Don't worry – this is a transient phase. Just stay calm and patient and avoid making a fuss.

To minimise the mess you have to clean up try the following:

★ Stand the high chair on a plastic tablecloth or newspaper to make floor cleaning easier.

★ Draw a circle on the high chair tray to show him where to put his cup. Or, until he learns to stop tipping his cup upside down, use a cup which has a mouthpiece.

★ If he gets very messy, make a game out of taking him to the sink to wash his hands.

★ Use a plate with deep sides and compartments so he can get the food up more easily with the fork, without using his hands.

★ Use a plastic bib with a large food-catching compartment.

FOOD ALLERGIES AND INTOLERANCES

Although often blamed for behavioural problems in children (see page 89), there is little evidence to support the theory that food allergies are the culprit. Food allergies are actually very rare in both children and adults and symptoms can be extreme, including headaches, skin rashes, vomiting and diarrhoea, and swelling of the mouth, tongue and face.

Food intolerances are more common and simply mean that a food doesn't suit you as well as some others. If your toddler consistently refuses a particular food, it may just be that it doesn't agree with him. Don't try and force him to eat it – substitute an equally nutritious food.

If you suspect your child has an allergy to any food type, then consult a paediatrician. Do not withdraw foods from his diet without advice as this could lead to nutritional deficiencies.

If your child has behavioural problems, consider all other causes, not just those related to food.

Very often a child is simply asking for some attention (for your toddler's emotional needs see pages 76–93).

DOS AND DON'TS WITH FEEDING

✔ Do keep reminding your child how bad sweets are for his teeth.
✔ Do be flexible with your child's eating habits.
✔ Do discourage friends and relatives from bringing junk food as gifts.
✘ Don't give into your child's demands for junk food.
✘ Don't use food as a reward or bribe or refuse it as punishment.
✘ Don't allow mealtimes to turn into battles.

Hygiene and bathing

Standards of hygiene are individual to each family. Some people believe that the house and children should be kept scrupulously clean to protect against infections; others take the view that a little bit of dirt never did anyone any harm.

It is impossible to protect your child from every illness and infection and in any case, she will need

A STEP UP
Position a standing block or small stepstool by the sink to make reaching the basin easier.

to build up her immunity against these. However, it is important to keep a balance between under- and over-protection while imparting personal hygiene rules to last her through life.

Children are particularly vulnerable to stomach upsets such as diarrhoea and vomiting, so you can help to combat this with good kitchen hygiene. Always store food safely and cook it thoroughly. Prepare food with clean utensils, in a clean environment.

At home

When your child begins feeding herself, get her into the habit of washing her hands before eating or touching food and teach her not to eat any fruit or raw vegetables before these have been washed. She should also learn to wash her hands after going to the toilet, playing outside or with pets. Supervise her hand washing until you are satisfied she is doing it properly.

Many toddlers rely on comfort blankets; if your child has one, don't allow her to trail it around and then suck it. Wash it frequently – if necessary when she's asleep and is less likely to miss it.

Outdoors

Toddlers who crawl or play on the ground tend to put dirty fingers in their mouths or eat dirt and are at particular risk from toxocariasis, a disease caused by roundworm infection. Toxocara eggs are found in the faeces of infected animals and may remain in the ground for two years or more. The disease can cause asthma, stomach upset and listlessness and even sight problems. Try to prevent your child eating dirt, sand or grass and discourage her from sucking dirty fingers. Keep her nails short to minimise dirt getting stuck under them. If you have a sandpit, always keep it covered when not in use. If you are out with your toddler, carry moist wipes to clean her hands.

Dos and don'ts with pets

✔ Do wash toys before giving them back to your child if a family pet gets hold of them.
✔ Do worm pets regularly and also check for fleas and ringworm, which can be passed on to children.
✘ Don't allow your child to kiss pets or any animal to lick your child's mouth.
✘ Don't let your pets eat from the same plates as humans.
✘ Don't let your child share her food or bed with a pet.

KEEPING CLEAN
Let your child do her own washing with soap and a flannel of her choice. Make sure she knows which tap is the cold one.

BATHTIME ROUTINE

As soon as your child is active she will probably need a daily bath to wash off any dirt acquired during play. Most toddlers love bathtime as it gives them an opportunity for waterplay. Let her play in the bath for as long as she wants. If she needs a bath when she wakes up, let her eat first as toddlers are usually starving when they awake.

Use bathtime to teach your child her body parts and how to wash herself. Name and point out parts, such as her feet or tummy, and give her a small sponge or flannel so she can wash these herself. Make sure your toddler knows which flannel and towel is hers – it is better for hygiene and it may encourage her to use them. Until she is old enough to wash herself thoroughly, you will have to go over what she has done.

Use mild soaps and shampoos as a toddler's skin is very sensitive. Try different brands to see what suits her skin best. Liquid soap may be easier for your toddler to handle.

AVOIDING PROBLEMS IN THE BATH

Some young toddlers dislike bathtime because they are frightened of being in the water. If your child develops a fear of bathtime, try making it more fun by adding a mild bubble bath, soap crayons, a selection of water toys, or singing appropriate nursery rhymes such as "rub a dub dub, three men in a tub". If your toddler is scared of getting her face wet, show her how to blow bubbles in the water. Taking her swimming or allowing her to play with the garden hosepipe may also help to overcome this fear.

Your child may feel more confident in the water if you join her in the bathtub. Let her splash you or pour water over your head, then do the same to her. Or, let her bathe with friends – it makes great fun for them. If she is really making a fuss about bathing, let her stand in a bowl of water while you wash her. Or, you can try taking her into the shower with you. If nothing else works, revert to sponge bathing until she feels ready to go back into the water.

SAFETY FIRST IN THE BATHROOM

▶ Never leave your toddler in the bath on her own, or leave any water standing in the tub.

▶ Make sure the water is a moderate temperature – no higher than 50°C (120°F); test it with your own foot before putting your child in.

▶ Store all medications including over-the-counter preparations, all electrical equipment, clippers, razors and scissors out of reach of your toddler.

▶ Make the bath slip-proof by using rubber strips or a rubber mat; use a non-skid bath mat to cover most of the bathroom floor (see page 52).

▶ Lock toilet bowl cleaner and other cleansers away.

▶ When not in use, keep the toilet lid closed with suction cups or a latch, if necessary.

HAIRCARE

Hair grows on average about a centimetre a month, but some children are still practically bald at 12 months, while others have a mop of hair that needs regular trimming.

LEARNING TO BRUSH
By 12 months your toddler will be keen to hold her brush and by age three she will have enough coordination to attempt to brush her hair but she will need your help to get it right.

WASHING

Hair washing can be difficult with toddlers as most young children hate getting water splashed near their faces and fear shampoo getting in their eyes.

To make washing your child's hair easier, wash it in the bath. Ask her to lie down so her hair gets wet in the water. Once she is sitting up again, quickly shampoo it, then use a spray attachment to rinse it, with your child's head tipped backwards. A plastic hairshield that fits around the hairline can also be worn by your child to stop water and shampoo running into her eyes.

Allowing your child some control over hairwashing may also help – let her wet her hair herself with a cloth or play a splashing game to see who can wet it first. You could also get in the bath and let her wash your hair first. If she is scared of getting her face wet, wet your face to show her there is nothing to worry about.

If nothing works and your child still struggles when having her hair washed, keep her hair short and sponge it regularly to keep it clean until she is more willing to have it washed.

Hair can be washed everyday with water or two to three times a week with baby shampoo.

BRUSHING

If you are letting your child's hair grow long, brush it regularly to keep it free from tangles. Be careful not to pull the hair too tightly if you are braiding it or putting it into bunches as this could cause thinning or permanent bald patches.

If your child's hair is long or curly, use conditioner after shampooing to prevent tangles. Don't rough towel dry the hair – rather pat it dry. If it is still tangled, use spray-on conditioner while combing it with a wide-toothed comb. This type of conditioner does not need to be washed out.

HEALTHY HAIR

Your toddler needs to get plenty of vitamins and minerals to ensure that her hair grows healthily. Possible problems with hair may include dandruff or cradle cap which can be treated with baby medicated shampoo or a shampoo for sensitive skin.

When she gets older and has more contact with other children she is at risk of catching head lice. These are easily removed with a special comb or chemical solution (see page 46).

FUSS-FREE CURLS
Using spray-on conditioner can help to minimise the after-bath tears as you try to get a comb through your toddler's hair.

TOOTHCARE

Most children have three or four teeth by the time they are 12 months old, and all 20 first (primary) teeth by the time they are three years old. However, some children do not have any teeth at all until after their first birthday.

Your child's first teeth are just as important as her permanent teeth and should be looked after properly. Decayed teeth will cause your child toothache and require fillings or removal. If the first teeth are lost too soon, the adjoining teeth may drift closer together, leaving less space for the permanent teeth to emerge. This can cause overcrowding or crooked permanent teeth, and your child may need braces or extractions later on.

TOOTH DECAY

When teeth are not cleaned properly, plaque – a combination of mucus, food and bacteria – builds up on the teeth. When the bacteria come into contact with food residue, particularly sugar, acid is produced. If it is not washed away, it attacks the tooth enamel, causing tiny holes or cavities which can lead to decay.

Fluoride strengthens the teeth and helps to prevent against decay. It is added to many brands of toothpaste and to water supplies in some areas. Fluoride supplements are available but should only be given to your child on the advice of your dentist or doctor. Too much in the long term can cause unsightly mottling. Children's fluoride toothpaste contains smaller amounts than ordinary fluoride toothpaste because children tend to swallow their toothpaste. Ask your dentist to recommend a toothpaste and how much to use.

BRUSHING HER TEETH

Start cleaning your child's teeth as soon as her first teeth emerge. The best way to do this with a young child is to sit with her on your lap, resting her head against your chest, or stand behind her and tilt her head upwards. Use a soft child-size toothbrush and no more than a small, pea-size amount of fluoride toothpaste. Brush the teeth in small circles covering the outer, inner and biting surfaces of the teeth, and covering the gums too. Rather than getting her to rinse with water, which reduces the benefit of fluoride, get her to just spit the paste out.

If your child is reluctant to let you brush her teeth, you can clean them by wrapping your finger over a piece of damp gauze with a tiny amount of fluoride toothpaste.

CLEANING HER OWN TEETH
Most children don't have the dexterity to clean their teeth properly until they reach ten, so you will need to supervise them.

DOS AND DON'TS WITH TEETH

✔ Do brush your child's teeth twice a day and after eating sugary foods.
✔ Do check food labels for sugars.
✔ Do buy sugar-free medicines.
✔ Do take your child for her first visit to the dentist by the time she is two.
✘ Don't let her fall asleep drinking juice from a bottle.
✘ Don't dip her dummy into anything sweet.
✘ Don't give her anything to eat or drink after the bed-time toothbrushing.

SLEEPING AND BEDTIME ROUTINES

From about 12–18 months of age your toddler will probably begin to need less sleep. One daytime nap is usually dropped as she starts to find far more exciting activities to do around the house. Night-time sleep problems may also begin as your toddler starts asserting her independence.

HOW MUCH SLEEP DOES A TODDLER NEED?

The amount of sleep a child needs varies; some children need more and others less. A bad temper and fretfulness can indicate a lack of sleep. Be realistic about how much sleep your own child needs. If your two-year-old only sleeps 11 hours at night, then it is unreasonable to put her to bed at seven in the evening and expect her to sleep through until eight the next morning. Generally, you can count on: 12–14 hours (including naps) for a one-year-old, 12–13 hours (including naps) for a two-year-old, and 12 hours for a three-year-old.

SHOULD TODDLERS TAKE NAPS?

Most toddlers have a nap in the day up to the age of two, and some may need a short sleep up to the age of three

or four. A nap will last however long your child needs to sleep, and usually occurs at a regular time each day. If your child naps at a time which is not convenient to you or so late in the afternoon that it makes bedtime too late, try to make her naptime 10–15 minutes earlier or later each day until she naps when you want her to.

Some toddlers will refuse to nap but may still need to have a rest. If this is the case with your child, allow her to play quietly with some toys in her bed or put on an audio story or music tape. Or you could use the opportunity to read to her.

To encourage your child to continue taking naps, you could try the following. Ease her away from over-strenuous activity some time before; offer her a soporific snack – milk and biscuits (unsweetened), for example; make sure her room is darkened, and settle her down much as for bedtime. If she's resisting a nap because she doesn't want to lose your company, spend a short time with her reading or just relaxing.

CHANGING FROM A COT TO A BED

The age you put your toddler into a bed is a matter for personal preference, but once she can climb over the top of a cot you may wish to put her into a single bed for safety reasons. She can

NIGHTLIGHTS

These come in various designs and can help your toddler overcome fear of the dark. The simplest ones plug directly into a wall outlet and give off a low-level illumination.

ALTERNATIVE TO A NAP
If your toddler won't sleep, quiet play in bed may help restore her.

easily hurt herself if she climbs over her cot's high rail. Most children will not object to changing over to a bed, but the occasional toddler may be reluctant to leave a familiar environment. If space isn't a problem, keep both the cot and the bed in the room for a few weeks so she can sleep part of the time in each.

Choose a time when your toddler is fairly settled – no new siblings, not getting over an illness or being toilet trained or weaned, and not just before going on holiday.

Your child will probably enjoy helping you to pick out new bedlinen but narrow down her choices in the shop or she'll soon become fractious. Always cover the new bed with plastic sheeting in case of accidents.

Transferring a favourite blanket can help acclimatise a toddler to a new bed, as will a selection of her favourite cot toys although she may prefer a new stuffed animal as a companion for her big bed.

The new bed should be low to the ground to prevent your toddler hurting herself should she fall out. You may also need to put guard rails down the sides or cushions alongside the bed until she gets used to it.

A BEDTIME ROUTINE

Establishing a simple and soothing bedtime routine for your toddler creates security and is the first step in preventing sleep problems. As far as

A GOOD NIGHT Making your child feel happy about going to bed is important if she's to stay there.

possible, try to keep to the routine, so that your child understands that it leads to going to bed and sleeping.

★ Set a time for your child to go to bed and make sure she does so regularly. Give her plenty of warning as bedtime approaches.

★ Bathe your toddler shortly before bedtime each night; allow her to play a little but don't let her get too excited.

★ Put her in her night clothes; give her a milky drink or snack before brushing her teeth.

★ Once she's in her bed, don't leave right away. Spend some quiet time with her – have a chat about the day's events or read her a story.

★ Tuck her up and give her a cuddle and a goodnight kiss. Leave the room before she's asleep.

SAFE AND SECURE With a little care and attention, you can ensure your child's room will not present any dangers. Install wall lights and avoid trailing electrical cords, cover outlets, put locks on windows, use stair guards, cover radiators and make sure furniture has rounded corners and secure knobs. A night-time potty may prevent accidents.

SLEEP PROBLEMS

Sleep problems are common in toddlers, although parents vary in their attitude to them. Some parents take it in their stride if their toddler refuses to go to bed or if she constantly wakes during the night and demands their attention. Other parents are driven to distraction by their toddler's bad sleeping habits and feel continually exhausted by broken nights.

If you and your partner are relaxed about your child's sleeping habits, then you needn't worry about what anyone else says. If, however, there is a problem you want to resolve, there are several management strategies which can be attempted. These will take time and patience and will need agreement and consistent behaviour on the part of both parents or anyone else involved. Your health visitor can give you more advice.

CRYING OR WAKING DURING THE NIGHT

Whenever your child is unwell or frightened, go into her bedroom and reassure her when she wakes up. If, however, she habitually cries after you have left the room or wakes during the night, leave her for a while before going back in. When you do go in, reassure her then say goodnight, making it clear that she is expected to stay in bed. If she is standing up on her bed when you enter, tuck her in again but keep talk to a minimum.

Do not spank or threaten her but also do not pick her up to cuddle her. Repeat this process for however long it takes, leaving longer intervals between the time she cries and the time you return. Don't reward her for waking up, by giving her a drink for example: to prevent her asking for a drink, leave one by the bed.

GETTING OUT OF BED

If your child repeatedly gets out of bed and comes into your room, tell her firmly that she has to go to bed and take her back. Ignore any crying and tell her she must stay in bed. Try not to get angry with her or give in. Repeat this process until your child gets

the message that you mean what you say. If she regularly gets up early, leave some toys for her to play with.

By the time your child reaches three years old, she should be learning to understand the concept of privacy and be less inclined to insist on waking you up early. To encourage this idea, give her her own personal space where she keeps her toys. Reaffirm that certain things, such as her clothes, belong only to her. In time she will respect your need to be left undisturbed.

NIGHTMARES AND NIGHT TERRORS

Most children experience frightening dreams at some time. Commonly, they begin between the ages of 18 months and three years. Nightmares are usually not a sign of emotional disturbance but may be sparked off by a disturbing television programme or a frightening story. If they occur very frequently, they may be a sign that your child is anxious or upset about something.

If your child has a nightmare she will need your comfort and reassurance. To help forestall bad dreams, it is a good idea to limit stimulation such as television viewing, loud music or noisy games before bedtime.

TEARFUL NIGHTS
It is important to try and resist the urge to pick up a wakeful toddler for a cuddle if you are going to train her to sleep through the night.

Occasionally, you may be wakened by your toddler giving a piercing scream or crying in fright and find her sitting up and staring in terror but still asleep. This is what is called a night terror. Your child is not aware of your presence and in the morning she will not remember the dream. During a night terror, the best thing to do is not to wake her but to tuck her up and stay with her until she falls into a calm sleep again.

FEAR OF THE DARK

As your child gets older, her imagination becomes more active and night-time can be frightening. Also, she may wake in the dark having to use the toilet. A nightlight, therefore, should be left on in the room or outside, with her door kept open but make sure it does not cast strange shadows.

Don't force your child to sleep in a dark room or lock her inside. This is particularly important when your child has to sleep in a strange bed, such as when visiting relatives or on holiday. Taking some favourite toys for the bed can help, as does your being close by. A toddler should never be left to sleep alone in a strange room.

NIGHT WANDERING

This unsupervised wandering about the house is a dangerous habit for your toddler to develop and should be discouraged. A sleeping bag, introduced during the first year, may help to prevent her from wandering. However, if the habit does arise, it may be difficult to break – but no matter how difficult keeping her in bed becomes, do not be driven to using physical restraints. This is potentially dangerous and teaches her that bedtime means imprisonment. If your child does wander, ensure that windows, external doors and entrances to the kitchen and bathroom are locked. Also you may want to place a gate across the top of the stairs.

The best deterrent is to ensure that she gains nothing from her exploits; if she appears in the living room, get her back to bed immediately and do not reward her with attention or this may become a nightly performance. Since you cannot force her to sleep, accept night waking and provide her with a night light and some toys.

BEDTIME SNACK
One cause of wakefulness during the night is hunger – if your child does get hungry during the night, give her a milky drink before brushing her teeth but avoid any sugary foods.

Overcoming sleep problems

- Try not to get too uptight about her sleepless-ness, as she will pick up on your anxiety.
- Be firm with your child – she needs her sleep and so do you. But don't view her behaviour as naughty – irritable children usually just want extra attention.
- Make sure she has plenty of fresh air and exercise during the day.
- Shorten her daytime naps or avoid late afternoon naps. If she is going to bed too late, start a routine that is ten minutes earlier each night.
- Let her sit with you and feel close to you and wait until her eyes start to droop before you take her to bed.
- Don't insist she goes to sleep straight away or send her to bed as a punishment.
- Never send your child to bed feeling unhappy, for example after you have scolded her.
- If she uses a dummy leave several in the bed so that she can find one if she wakes up. Make sure she has any other comforters, such as a favourite toy.
- Make sure her bedroom is warm.
- Play soft music on a tape or the radio.
- Try to find out if anything is bothering your child – persistent crying may indicate that she is worried about something.
- Give an older toddler a reward for not waking you up, such as a star chart.

CLOTHES AND SHOES

Although you may wish to dress your child in a pretty frilly dress or a smart suit for special occasions, day-to-day wear for toddlers should be comfortable, practical and easy to wash. It is natural for children to get dirty when playing and concerns from you about keeping clothes clean can spoil your child's enjoyment of play. If your child is painting or playing with water, a protective apron can be worn.

T-shirts or sweaters with dungarees or coveralls, are ideal for toddlers who are still in nappies and at the climbing stage. For outdoors or if she is playing in the garden, a warm washable jacket with a hood (but no strings) is very handy.

In wet or cold weather, a padded one-piece weatherproof suit (snowsuit) is useful. This should be large enough to go over other clothing and to give your child plenty of freedom to move.

Young children outgrow their clothes very quickly and it is best to buy clothes that are

DOS AND DON'TS WITH CLOTHES

✔ Do buy clothes that are flame resistant.

✔ Do buy practical and hard wearing clothes.

✔ Do buy loose and comfortable clothes that are easy to put on and take off.

✔ Do buy clothes that are easy to wash.

✘ Don't buy clothes that have any strings in the hood or around the neck, as these could get caught and strangle your child.

✘ Don't buy the smallest size, even if these are a 'bargain'.

FASHION CHOICE
Choosing her own clothes will give your toddler the opportunity to practise talking, and learn about colours and the names of clothing. It may also encourage her to learn to dress herself and be more independent.

slightly bigger than their size, rather than getting their actual size. Watch out for clothes sales and buy larger sizes to keep for when your child gets bigger.

On a hot summer's day, make sure that your child's clothes adequately protect the back of her neck and shoulders against the sun (see page 54).

Once your child is starting to be toilet trained, choose clothes that are easy to pull down – for example, trousers with an elasticated waist and without any awkward zips or buttons.

NIGHTCLOTHES
In some countries, such as Britain, children's nightclothes are required to be made from low flammability materials, that is, material which is slow to burn. Sleepsuits are ideal for young toddlers. As your child gets older, he or she can progress to nightdresses or pyjamas.

Whatever you choose, cotton is best, especially if your child has sensitive skin, or a skin problem such as eczema.

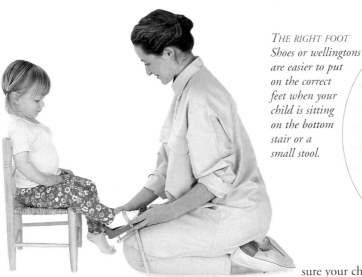

CORRECT FIT
Your toddler's shoes must be correctly fitted to prevent
damage to her feet and poor development. Make sure
you go to a shoe store with a trained fitter.

SHOES

Once your child is walking outdoors and her feet
need some protection, making sure she wears
correctly fitting shoes is essential. A child's foot is
wide at the toes and slimmer at the heels and
there is little hard bone – just cartilage and gristle.
As a result, pressure from ill-fitting shoes and
socks can distort the shape of the foot, especially
in the early years, and may cause permanent
damage. Also, because there is so little bone in a
child's foot, she may not complain about ill-fitting
shoes hurting. Your child's shoes should therefore
be fitted individually by a trained shoe fitter and
should never be bought second-hand or passed
down from older siblings.

The type of shoes you buy for your child should
be designed around the shape of the foot and
should be the correct width as well as the correct
size. Materials should be natural, such as leather,
cotton or canvas to allow sweat to escape and the
foot to 'breathe'. The shoes should have plenty of
room at the front to allow the toes to grow, and
be firm and snug at the heel to cradle the foot
without restriction or slipping.

Although sandals are cooler in the summer, if
they are not fitted properly they may harm your
child's feet as they tend to slip easily and are not
easy to run in. Your child will curl her toes in as
she tries to prevent them slipping – this will
prevent the feet from developing properly. Make
sure your child is professionally fitted for
sandals.

As children find it easier to use buckles or press
velcro straps than tying knots in laces, buy these
types of shoes first.

Because children's feet grow so quickly, there is
no point buying expensive shoes. In fact, you
should check that they still fit every two months.
You can expect to buy new shoes for your toddler
every four to six months until the age of five.

Whenever it is safe to do so, let your child walk
barefoot as this will help her feet develop.

SOCKS

Socks should always be pure cotton and not
acrylic or wool, to enable feet to breathe properly
and to minimise the possibility of fungal
infections.

Correct-fitting socks are as important as shoes
and should be chosen with the same care. If they
are too big, they can ruin a correctly fitted shoe
by causing pressure; if they are too small they will
scrunch the toes and discourage straight growth.
Make sure you check regularly that your child's
socks still fit her.

CHILD WATCH

- Make sure an area is safe before
letting your child run around barefoot. Broken glass or
sharp pebbles can cause serious injuries.
- Always wash and dry your child's feet thoroughly to
minimise the chance of skin infections such as fungal
infections. Make sure you dry properly between her toes.
- Keep toe nails short to prevent them digging into
shoes. Cut them with gentle curves – sharp
corners may become ingrown.

DRESSING AND SELF-DRESSING

By the age of 15 months, your child will be taking the first steps towards dressing independently. You may also find it difficult to get her to stay still long enough for you to dress her! If your toddler is reluctant to get dressed, try making a game of it, such as hide and seek: 'where's your head gone then? oh, there it is' when you pull a sweater over her head. If she refuses to put her coat on when going out, take it with you and offer it to her after a few minutes outside. If she is cold she is likely to accept it.

Singing can also help a reluctant toddler to get dressed. Try the song below or make up your own. Encourage your child to sing along with you. If your child is cross in the morning, let her have her breakfast before you get her dressed.

At 18 months, your toddler may find it fun to discard her clothes, including her nappy, shoes and socks, having discovered how to do this. But she will also be learning how to cooperate, such as raising her arms for a sweater.

When you dress your young toddler it is a good opportunity to teach her the body parts, what the clothes are, where they go, why you are putting them on, and what they do. This will also help her to learn to dress independently. For example 'shirt over vest', 'trousers over pants,' 'snowsuit keeps you warm and dry', 'zipper keeps snowsuit zipped', 'hat goes on head', 'scarf keeps neck warm', ' mitts keep your hands warm', 'boots keep feet dry', and so on.

Very young children don't mind what they wear. But by the age of three, your child may have very definite likes and dislikes and may make a great fuss about certain clothes. As far as practicable, let her choose what to wear and don't criticise her choice. Tact may be needed however, if she refuses to wear a garment that grandma made!

MAKING DRESSING EASIER

Although you can do the job more quickly yourself, learning to dress herself is an important step in your child learning to become independent and self-reliant. Don't expect too much at first but offer a hand if she wants this. Try not to interfere or laugh if your child gets it wrong, otherwise she may become very cross or discouraged. Even if you don't like her choice of colours, do allow her some independence at this stage. Don't fight with your child about clothes.When she is old enough, let her select what clothes she wants to wear from a suitable range of summer or winter clothes.

Lay out the clothes in a way that your child can go up to them and put them on easily. For example, if the clothes have a picture on the front, place these downwards so that they are facing away from her when she puts them on. If there are buttons on the back of the garment, place these facing upwards. Lay out trousers with the waist closest and the front upmost.

Put a vest or sweater down with the head furthest away and teach her how to burrow into these from the bottom.

Let's put on your special top,
Your special top, your special top.
Let's put on your special top
Let's put the top on you.
Let's put on your special socks,
Your special socks, your special socks.
Let's put on your special socks
Let's put the socks on you.

(Your special shirt, shoes, coat etc.)

SINGALONG
Singing this song to your toddler as you dress her may make a daily chore into a game she looks forward to. It works well to the tune of 'Here we go round the mulberry bush'.

A 'learning to dress' doll can give your child practice in doing up buttons, laces, zips and velcro straps.

FASTENINGS

When your toddler is learning how to use a zip, teach her to pull this away from the skin and clothes to prevent catching. When she is being toilet trained, buy trousers with elasticated waists that are easy to pull up and down. Velcro fasteners are also easy to manage as are dungarees with hooks, not buttons. When she does learn to use buttons, teach her to button from the bottom upwards – this will help to avoid getting the buttons in the wrong holes.

POSSIBLE PROBLEMS WITH DRESSING YOUR TODDLER

Some toddlers develop such an enthusiasm for dressing themselves that they will refuse your help, even when you are in a hurry to go out. Although this can be frustrating for you, it is best to leave as much time as you can to enable your toddler to dress herself – you will appreciate her independence in later years. Interfering and trying to take over what she wants to do herself will take away her pleasure in learning.

A fussy toddler can also be a handful if she refuses to wear what is appropriate for the climate and the activity she will be doing that day. To minimise arguments, only put those clothes which you want her to wear in accessible drawers. You will also have to be firm when she is being really difficult – threatening to leave her at home while you go out often gets her dressed quickly, but she will probably realise at some point that you are only bluffing.

EFFORTS NOT WASTED!
Even though your toddler may make several frustrated attempts before she gets it right, if she is enjoying the experience of trying to get dressed, give her as much time as she needs.

PULL YOUR SOCKS UP
You could help your toddler to get her socks on by pulling them over her heels, as this is the most difficult part for her to do.

THE MISSING HEAD
Asking your toddler where her head is will provide entertainment time and time again until she is mature enough to realise how silly you are!

ZIPPING UP
Take special care to show your little boy how to do up a zipper safely to avoid nasty nips of the penis.

DAILY ROUTINES

During these toddler years, your child will progress from the baby who was fully dependent on you to a person in her own right – and one beginning to assert her independence. Although you cannot change the sequence in which develop-mental changes occur, you can help your child to master each new skill and thus help her to achieve her full potential.

PROMOTING DEVELOPMENT

The stages your child will grow through in becoming an independent person who is manually adept and capable of confident locomotion and fluid communication are known as developmental milestones. Provided they are healthy and in a nurturing environment, the majority of children will reach these recognised stages by certain ages (see below).

your child to achieve her maximum, but try not to compare her progress with that of other children. Let her go at her own pace. Your neighbour's child may be walking while your child is still crawling, or your child may be saying more words than a playmate who is two months older. Yet all these children will be developing normally.

There are three main areas to monitor. These are physical development, including locomotive and manipulative skills; mental development, which focuses on the ability to think and communicate; and social development, learning to relate to and interact with others. The pattern of development proceeds in the same sequence for all children – for example, your child has to learn to stand before she can walk, but there is wide variety in the rate of development. You should encourage

As you watch your child develop in these toddler years and help her to cope with the many changes that occur, you will inevitably experience lots of different emotions. There is bound to be some sadness that your baby is starting to grow up, frustration when she tests your patience to the limits in her bids to achieve independence, and lots of happiness and pride in her achieve-ments and in her obvious delight in new-found abilities.

There also will be a welcome increase in

communication between the two of you. This should be nutured as it can only help you to help your child achieve her goals.

INTELLECTUAL DEVELOPMENT

Also known as 'cognitive' or 'mental' development, intellectual development includes the mastery of communication skills, particularly speech; using the imagination; remembering things; learning new skills such as reading, drawing and counting; learning what things are and how they work different colours, and so on. There are a number of ways in which you can promote your child's intellectual development.

Language
★ Always look at your child when talking to her and use short, simple sentences.

★ Listen to your child when she is talking, and allow her to finish off sentences.
★ Encourage your child to hold a conversation with her doll or teddy. Pretend play will help her linguistic and creative development.
★ When out with your child describe things to her. For example, 'there's a red car', 'that's a big dog'.
★ Look at books with her and point out what the characters are doing.
★ Expand on what your child says. For example, if she says 'keys' tell her; 'the keys go in the door' or when she says 'bye-bye', add 'bye-bye granny.'
★ Encourage your child to listen to different sounds but don't let her be subjected to a continual barrage such as leaving the radio or television on all day. Use programmes occasionally as a basis for conversation, but have some 'quiet times' with her such as reading and holding conversations together.

MILESTONES IN INTELLECTUAL DEVELOPMENT

15–18 MONTHS

★ Points to familiar objects in books.
★ Says six to 20 words. 'No' may start to become a favourite word.
★ Understands simple questions and instructions such as 'where are your shoes?', 'close the door', 'give it to me'.
★ May know two or three body parts such as the eyes and nose.
★ Imitates gestures.
★ Repeats own name.

TWO YEARS

★ Uses 50 or more words and may be putting two or three words together.
★ Understands longer instructions such as 'put the cup on the table'.
★ Understands simple short stories and conversations.
★ Uses pronouns such as 'me', 'you', 'I'. Begins to ask questions.

THREE YEARS

★ Knows two or three colours and some shapes.

★ Carries on a simple conversation and talks and asks 'where', 'what' and 'why' questions incessantly.
★ Will now understand more complicated sentences such as: 'go upstairs to your bedroom and fetch your coat from the wardrobe'.
★ May be able to count up to ten.
★ Will start understanding concepts such as yesterday and tomorrow.
★ Knows some nursery rhymes.

COUNTING
Use every opportunity to encourage your child to practise his counting. When he is done with his fingers, move on to his toes!

Colour knowledge

★ Teach your child about colours when doing household activities. For example, tell her you're cooking in a blue saucepan, vacuuming a red carpet, or potting a green plant.

★ When dressing her, tell her the colour of her clothes. For example, 'Let's put on your red skirt and your white t-shirt'.

★ Tell her about colours outside – the sky is blue, the dog is black, the flowers are pink and yellow, the grass is green and so on.

Counting

★ Sing rhymes such as 'One, two three four, five, once I caught a fish alive', or 'One, two, buckle my shoe', and play lots of counting games.

★ As soon as your child can walk upstairs holding your hand, count the steps as you go up.

★ Tell her about numbers when you are doing things, for instance that you are laying two knives and forks on the table or buying four apples.

★ Count out the parts of the body: ten fingers, ten toes, one nose, one mouth and two eyes, and one belly button.

Memory

★ Talk about and remind her of things which she has seen and done during the day. For example, if she saw a big bus or went on the swings, ask her if she can remember what colour the bus was, or what she did in the park.

SPEECH PROBLEMS

As children start to use words it is natural for them to mispronounce some or substitute some sounds and develop a lisp: for example, 'w' for 'r' (wed for red) or 'f' for 'th' (fum for thumb). As her speech increases and she has so much to say, your child may also sound as if she is developing a stutter or stammer. Sometimes too, a hearing impairment may be the cause of slow or poor speech development (see page 38).

Try not to correct any mistakes directly, laugh, or draw attention to her speech as your child may then become self-conscious about talking and develop a real stammer. Instead, it is better to repeat what she has said, but emphasise the correct pronunciation of the word. For example, 'Yes, that's right, it's a red ball'. Given time and encouragement, most children do learn to speak in the correct way, but if you have any serious concerns about your child's speech, then talk to your doctor or health visitor.

Lateness in acquiring speech This is more common in boys than girls and is often a familiar characteristic; check if you or your partner was a late speaker. Children learn most from their parents and the commonest cause for lack of speech is if a parent doesn't speak or sing to a child often enough. Once speech is attempted it should be actively encouraged even if it is imprecise. Deafness can also result in late speech – make sure you test your child's hearing.

Frustration with speech acquisition Learning how to communicate is a very important step in your toddler's development. She is learning to say words, as well as to express her thoughts and feelings. It is only natural for your child to get

CHILD WATCH
Talk to your doctor if:
By 15–18 months your child:
• Does not say any single words at all.
• Does not understand very simple sentences.
• Often appears uninterested and unresponsive.
• Does not appear to hear sounds.

By two years your child:
• Does not join two words.

By three years your child:
• Does not speak so you can understand her.
• Does not make a three word sentence.

frustrated as she is learning to say what she wants, and to perhaps express this through screaming or a temper tantrum (see page 80).

DEVELOPMENT OF LOCOMOTION

Your child's journey to full independent locomotion began when he first was able to hold his neck steady as an infant. Though he may still be wobbly on his feet, over the next few years he will continue to acquire skills that will enable him to become master of his home and outdoor environment, as well as engage in various kinds of play and sporting activities.

Your child will have boundless energy, and your main priority will be to divert this into safe physical activities, which will enable him to practise these new skills and thus help him to develop. As well as using up some of his energy, walking, running and jumping will also exercise his body and help build coordination between his brain and limbs. You may find parent and toddler gym classes are available in your area, or you may need to organise physical activities for your toddler at home, or in the local park.

Some children are more graceful in their movements and more efficient in skills such as kicking a ball than others. Some children are also less dextrous than others, and for example, may not be good at building things. Some clumsiness is also natural when your child first starts developing his physical skills – it will take some time before he becomes surefooted and you should not worry if he bumps into things or trips. If you are worried that there is a serious problem, see a doctor – it is likely that any problem will be minor and easily corrected.

MILESTONES IN LOCOMOTIVE DEVELOPMENT

15–18 MONTHS

★ Walks alone.
★ Kneels and crawls upstairs on all fours.
★ Walks upstairs by holding on to the rail and putting both feet on each step.
★ Squats down or bends over to pick up a toy without falling.
★ Climbs furniture.
★ Waves bye-bye.

TWO YEARS

★ Runs.
★ Walks backwards.
★ Kicks a ball without falling over.
★ Walks on tip-toe.
★ Walks up and down steps with two feet per stair.

THREE YEARS

★ Can stand on one leg and hop.
★ Walks upstairs with one foot to each stair.
★ May jump from bottom step.
★ Can jump with two feet.
★ Rides a tricycle with feet on the pedals.
★ Dances to music.

Promoting your child's physical development

★ Let your child go for short walks without his pushchair. Give him the freedom to wander but supervise him closely.

★ Let him practise walking backwards by playing games that use backward steps.

★ Take him to safe open spaces. Play chasing games, or organise races.

★ Teach him to bend his knees to pick things up and to sit down backwards on a chair. Let him practise kicking and throwing a ball. Later you can help him practise balancing by holding his fingertips as he walks along the top of something safe such as a low wall or narrow steps.

★ Encourage your child to learn to jump by dancing to music with him. He will also enjoy 'bouncing' on his bed or on an old mattress, foam rubber, cushions or a small trampoline. As he gets older he will enjoy jumping and somersaulting over cushions or other safe objects.

★ Climbing gives your child the opportunity to use his muscles, gain control over his movements and help his balance. Climbing frames and slides will give him the opportunity to practise.

★ Large motor skills can be perfected through playing outside, and using push-along toys and ride-on toys.

SAFETY AWARENESS

Keep close at hand as your child begins to become more mobile – a new walker is an unsteady one and you should make sure that the floor is not too slippery. Also, avoid making him wear shoes until he is walking outside as he will find it easier to get around if he can feel the surface of the floor under his feet. But do make sure there is nothing sharp lying on the floor that he might walk on.

As his development progresses, sometimes quite rapidly, it may be difficult to keep track of what your child is capable of doing. He will be able to

SUCCESS AT LAST
Climbing furniture often becomes a favourite activity after the age of about 15 months. Toddlers are usually very creative in their attempts and, at first, will climb on facing forwards and then turn around.

climb up to things that were previously safely out of his reach and you will need to supervise him closely at all times.

Also, keep sharp objects and poisonous substances in places which you are sure are inaccessible to your child and try to establish safe areas in which he can play.

MANIPULATION

Hand-eye coordination is involved in a lot of the physical skills that your child needs to learn. As her manipulative skills improve she will be able to use her hands and fingers for activities such as building bricks, turning pages of a book, drawing, writing, combing her hair, doing up buttons, and using a spoon and fork. Manipulative skills have to be learned so it is important to give your child the opportunity to practise these over and over again.

Promoting manipulation

★ Show her how to unscrew lids, thread things on string or laces, pour water, turn pages of a book, rip paper, and so on.
★ Teach her how to do things for herself such as using a spoon and taking her socks off.
★ Give her activity boards, which contain spinning, twisting, dialling and turning features.
★ Provide her with building blocks and stacking toys.
★ Work at puzzles, drawing and painting together using a variety of pens, crayons and brushes.

MILESTONES IN MANIPULATIVE DEVELOPMENT

15–18 MONTHS

★ Can build a tower of three bricks.
★ Has started to scribble, scribbling more vigorously as she gets older.
★ Can take a cup to her mouth without spilling.
★ Feeds herself with a spoon without losing too much food.
★ Takes her socks off.
★ Can do simple puzzles.

TWO YEARS

★ Can turn door handles.
★ Turns the pages of a book over properly.
★ Can put on gloves, shoes and socks.
★ Threads beads, fastens buttons and a zip.
★ Can unscrew lids from jars.

THREE YEARS

★ Begins to dress and undress with help.
★ Can build a tower of nine bricks.
★ Draws circles and copies a cross if shown.
★ Eats with a fork and spoon.
★ Holds a pen properly.
★ Can pick up small objects.
★ Using both hands, she can pour water from a jug into a cup, usually without too much spillage.

DEVELOPING SOCIABILITY

The development of social skills and behaviour is important for your toddler's eventual emergence as an independent individual. Such skills include the ability to meet, mix and communicate with other people; learning how to play, share, take turns with others and accept rules; mastering toilet training and adhering to general standards of cleanliness and eating in 'acceptable' ways. As your child acquires these social skills she will also gain independence and confidence and learn to value herself and others.

HELLO AND GOODBYE
Always make sure you introduce your toddler to adults outside the family. Teach him to greet and say goodbye to visitors to your house.

IT'S MINE
Your toddler may 'hang on' to her toys or howl with rage if another child tries to grab them, or if you try to give them to another child.

Learning how to make friends and get on with people is an essential part of growing up. A child who is friendly and well liked is more self confident, and has more fun and play opportunities. Not every child is naturally confident and outgoing however and, like everything else, the ability to make friends and socialise has to be learnt. For the first two years your child will also be 'egocentric', that is, the centre of her own world. She is unable to understand the concept of sharing or the feelings of others and playing with other children often leads to tears over a coveted toy.

EMPATHY AND PERSONALITY

During the toddler years, as her self-knowledge grows, your child should begin to demonstrate that she is aware that what she feels is felt by others. She may even respond to another person's distress by becoming distressed herself. Empathy may encourage a child to become more generous and unselfish in play with others and is something you should try to help her to develop.

While aspects of your child's personality may have been apparent at birth (whether she cried a lot or was placid, for example) between the ages of two to three her personality will become quite manifest. It is likely that you will begin to have a clear idea of your child's personality such as whether she is bossy or adventurous.

While she has been learning to master the various locomotive and manipulative skills, she will experience determination and become aware of her ability to influence the actions of herself and others.

When she is unsuccessful in her attempts, she also will suffer from shame and failure. She must learn to handle both her successes and her failures in acceptable ways in order to become well-balanced.

You can help your child to better integrate the different aspects of personality – activity, sociability and emotionality – by showing her how to tackle problems successfully, distracting her when she becomes frustrated, and by enabling her to construct a positive self-image through praise without ridiculing her fears.

PROMOTING SOCIAL SKILLS

★ Involve your toddler with other children as much as you can by inviting other children to your house or by joining a 'parent and toddler' group.

★ Encourage loving behaviour towards other people, animals and dolls.

★ Take her on outings using public transport, and to public places such as the supermarket and cafés where she will learn to queue and wait for her turn.

★ If there is a dispute over a toy, try not to intervene immediately, but stand by to sort out any fights and introduce the idea of sharing and taking turns.

★ As soon as your child becomes old enough to understand, praise any attempts at sharing. At first she may share just to please you, rather than out of any sense of fairness. Introduce techniques such as each child taking turns to play with a favourite toy. You could set an alarm clock to ring every five minutes or so.

★ Teach her to say please and thank-you at the appropriate times.

RIGHT AND WRONG

By the age of three you need to make sure that your toddler is aware of the difference between 'good' and 'bad' actions. Try and explain to your toddler in simple ways why you want her to do one thing and not another. Most children like to do what is right, although it doesn't always stop them being naughty, since it is a way of getting you to pay attention to them.

Rather than concentrating on the negative aspects of personality, the best tack is to use positive reinforcement as much as possible. Give praise when your toddler is careful in situations or with others' feelings.

Many toddlers mix make-believe and reality or tell you things that are not strictly true. This is not lying but a natural part of behaviour at this age – some psychologists believe that children are only capable of lying after the age of four.

Some children constantly use the word 'no' even when they mean 'yes' but this is simply their way of trying to assert authority.

PROBLEMS WITH SOCIABILITY

Some children have trouble focusing their attention on anything for any length of time, including playing with other children. Others go through a phase of temper tantrums, aggressiveness, extreme insecurity or rapid and frequent mood changes (see pages 80–85). Often this is a natural stage of development and you need not worry. However, if your child's 'bad' behaviour is prolonged or you are having trouble coping with it ask your doctor or health visitor for some advice.

Autism This rare disorder is often detected by parents before a child reaches three. Characterised by an inability to relate to people and an obsessive resistance to change, it is physiological in origin and cannot be 'cured', although it is experienced in different degrees and, with treatment, can be modified. Consult your doctor if your child seems unaffectionate in the extreme, doesn't communicate well, or if he engages in very repetitive behaviour.

MILESTONES IN SOCIAL PLAY

15–18 MONTHS

★ Solitary play: at this age children usually prefer to play alone.

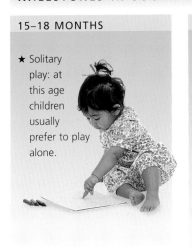

TWO YEARS

★ Spectator play: children enjoy watching other children play and are curious about them, however they are likely to play near them but not with them.

THREE YEARS

★ Joining-in play: children begin to play with other children and are learn-ing about sharing.

TOILET TRAINING: THE POTTY

Using the potty or toilet is a social and physical skill that your child needs to learn, although there is no magic age when all children become trained. On average, most children are dry during the day between the ages of two and three. Generally, bowel control is learnt before bladder control because the physical urge to pass water is more urgent and immediate.

STEPS IN BLADDER CONTROL

★ Your child goes for longer periods without a wet nappy. This indicates that the bladder has grown and has a larger storage capacity.
★ Your child is aware of passing urine and indicates to you that he is wet (or dirty), is wetting himself or is about to wet himself.
★ He is able to tell you in time to fetch the potty or to be put on the potty or toilet seat.
★ He is able to use the potty or go to the toilet himself.
★ He becomes dry during the day.
★ He becomes dry during the night.

Until your child is ready, trying to teach him potty training may result in frustration and frayed tempers for you, anxiety for your child, and a lot of hard work for nothing. In order to become clean and dry, your child's nervous system must be sufficiently mature for him to recognise the signs of a full bladder and bowel. He then needs to be able to control the muscles that open the bladder and bowel long enough to get to the potty before emptying them. This rarely happens before the age of 15–18 months.

WHEN TO BEGIN TRAINING

Eighteen months is the earliest age to start toilet training, with around two years the most realistic age. There are no hard-and-fast rules, but girls may be more ready from about 18 months, and boys nearer to 30 months.

It is too soon to start before 18 months but you can, if you wish, get your toddler used to sitting on the potty from around 15 months. Your child may empty his bowel after a meal but 'catching' a motion at this age is not toilet training but an involuntary reflex action. Don't force him to use the potty or leave him on it for more than a few moments. If he gets bored or cries, let him

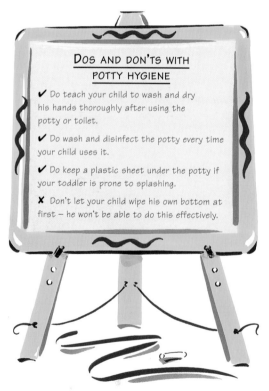

DOS AND DON'TS WITH POTTY HYGIENE

✔ Do teach your child to wash and dry his hands thoroughly after using the potty or toilet.

✔ Do wash and disinfect the potty every time your child uses it.

✔ Do keep a plastic sheet under the potty if your toddler is prone to splashing.

✘ Don't let your child wipe his own bottom at first – he won't be able to do this effectively.

MAKE IT EASY FOR HIM
Dress your toddler in clothes that are easy to remove and as few as possible. If you have a large home or rooms on several floors, have more than one potty in accessible places.

get off. If he does pass a motion, praise him, but don't comment if he doesn't.

Whatever age you decide to start training your child, choose a period when you can give him the time and encouragement needed. If there is a distraction, such as going on holiday, moving house, or you have just had another baby, then leave potty training until things have settled down. It is also easier in warm weather when your child has less clothes to cope with.

GETTING STARTED

Begin by explaining in simple language what you want him to do. Teach him what words to use when he needs to pass water or open his bowels. Let him know that it's a good thing to pooh or wee in a potty. It may be a good idea to let him pick a potty in his favourite colour. Make sure it has a rigid base to stop it tipping over and that there are no rough edges. For a boy, buy one with a splash guard.

Keep the potty in the same place, where he can get to it easily, and where it won't topple over. If you have an upstairs and downstairs, it is a good idea to have potties in different parts of the house. Make sure the area where he uses it is warm.

Dress him in clothes that are easy to take off and teach him how to pull his clothes down. Trainer pants may be useful and are easier to remove than nappies. They may also make your child feel more 'grown up'. Later on, let him go with you to choose his own knickers or underpants to wear.

Put him on the potty regularly, such as after meals and before going out, and stay with him in the early stages. Encourage your toddler to sit for a few minutes – let him look at a book or read him a story. If he sees you sitting on the toilet he may catch on more quickly.

If you have a boy, don't insist that he stands to wee – it is usually easier to sit at first. If he wants to stand, let him use a block to reach the bowl. When your child uses the potty successfully, give him some praise and encouragement – but not too much. If he doesn't get a result next time, he may become disappointed. Don't expect results too soon and don't nag or force the issue. Expect the occasional accident even after you think your child has become dry and be matter of fact about cleaning him up.

If your child fails to perform, refuses to use the potty, or wets himself, don't get angry. If he becomes anxious about toilet training and there is a battle between you and your child, put the potty away for a week or two or until your child is more ready. Never nag your toddler or force him to sit on the potty.

MAKE IT FUN FOR HIM
Although it is a good idea to encourage him to use the potty after meals and before bed, let him come and go as he pleases. If you place books or toys nearby, he will be encouraged to stay as long as necessary – but don't force him to stay on the potty.

GIVE HIM YOUR SUPPORT
Be enthusiastic when he is successful and relaxed when he makes a mistake.

Using the toilet

As your child gets older, you will need to teach him to use the toilet. (Some children who start training later may insist on using one from the start.) Letting your child copy you using it will get him used to the idea.

It is important that your child feels safe and secure when sitting on the toilet and you may find a special child's lavatory seat useful. Your child will also need a sturdy stepstool or box in order to reach the seat and to rest his feet on. Boys may also need a step when standing up to wee.

Some children are afraid of falling down the hole; if this is the case with your toddler, you will need to hold him on at first.

You should help your child get used to using other people's toilets by letting him use them when you are out visiting. You should also take him to toilets in public places. Show him how to use the various toilet paper dispensers but carry sufficient tissues in case they are lacking. Make sure your child understands that extra care of hygiene must be taken in public toilets. Teach him to check that the seat is dry and to wipe it down with toilet paper if necessary. Make sure he washes his hands extra thoroughly afterwards.

DOS AND DON'TS WITH TOILET TRAINING

✔ Do let your child choose his own toilet seat.
✔ Do let him flush the toilet if he wants to.
✔ Do ensure he washes his hands thoroughly every time.
✔ Do make sure girls wipe from front to back.
✗ Don't compare your child's progress with other children.

GROWING UP
Most children can't wait to progress from their potty to the 'big people's toilet' but they may need a little help up.

GOING THROUGH THE NIGHT
Learning to stay dry throughout the night usually takes children a little longer than staying dry during the day. Your child has to recognise the feeling of a full bladder while asleep and respond either by 'holding on' until morning or waking up and going to the toilet. About a quarter of three-year-olds wet the bed and need to wear a nappy, so don't be in any hurry to remove the plastic sheet and try not to lose your patience with frequent night accidents.

You can make it easier for your child to stay dry at night by making sure he doesn't have fizzy drinks, citrus juices or drinks with caffeine such as tea, cola and chocolate before going to bed. These can stimulate the kidneys to produce more fluid. Don't reduce the amount your child drinks, however, as the bladder tends to adjust and holds less fluid. It is better for your child to drink around six or seven cups of fluid during the day so that his bladder learns to hold a larger capacity.

You can help your child and minimise your own work by putting a small rubber sheet on top of the child's ordinary sheet with a half sheet over that. If there is an accident, you can quickly remove the half sheet and spare the rest of the undersheet. Most importantly, stay calm and don't make a big deal about it.

Up to the age of five, bed wetting is considered normal and treatment is not usually given. It may be discouraging to change wet beds but you should try not to get angry with your toddler. Putting a potty in the room may help and you should make sure he isn't afraid to get up at night, for instance by installing a nightlight. Don't let your child get constipated, as this can also irritate the bladder at night.

POSSIBLE PROBLEMS

★ Fear of flushing is very common and can cause problems with toilet training. Forcing your toddler to confront his fear will often make it worse. Let him acclimatise to flushing gradually; flush the toilet when he is out of the room but within earshot. When this no longer worries him, try holding him in the door way while the toilet is flushed. Try doing this nearer and nearer to the toilet until he is ready to pull the lever himself. Your toddler may actually fear flushing away a part of himself. Waving goodbye to the stool before you flush the toilet may help.

★ For some children fear of the toilet results in 'holding on', particularly to bowel movements, resulting in constipation (see page 45). For others it may lead to passing bowel movements in their pants or on the floor. If this is the case with your child, don't insist that he use the toilet, just let him use the potty until he is ready to give it up. Also, give him privacy in the bathroom as he may feel self-conscious, although you should make sure he can't lock himself in. Let him take as long as he needs to go. He could read a book if he wants to – this may help him to relax.

★ A previously toilet trained child may regress and start to pass motions in the wrong place; this may be due to physical illness or an emotional upheaval, for example following the arrival of a new sibling (see page 90) or moving house. This will usually resolve itself in its own time. It is important that you stay calm and don't make a fuss about it as it is likely your child is feeling insecure.

★ Your toddler may develop a fascination with his stool – to him a bowel movement is a remarkable achievement of which he may be very proud. If you discover your child playing with the contents of the potty or toilet, stay calm and do not make him feel ashamed of what he's done but explain that this is not acceptable for many reasons, including hygiene. Tell him that his stool belongs in the toilet or potty and must stay there until it is flushed away. Divert him from further interest by providing materials for more acceptable creative play, such as finger painting or playing with plasticine. If you find it impossible to divert him, consult your health visitor.

★ At some stage, your toddler will most probably develop an interest in how the opposite sex urinate. A girl may want to stand while it is difficult to persuade a boy to do so. In this instance it is best for instruction to come from the parent of the same sex as they will know best how to describe it. Explain the reason for the sitting/standing policy (a boy's stream aims out and a girl's down). If your little girl, for example, persists on trying to stand, let her have a go. Be on hand to clean up the mess at first but after a few tries she will probably discover the disadvantages for herself and her curiosity will be satisfied.

TRAINING PANTS
By three years your child should stay dry during the day but may need training pants to help him through the night.

MILESTONES IN TOILET TRAINING

15–18 MONTHS	TWO YEARS	THREE YEARS
★ Your child is likely to indicate that he has a wet or soiled nappy.	★ Your child is likely to indicate his toilet needs most of the time.	★ Your child is likely to be dry during the day and some nights.

Talk to your doctor or health visitor if by three years your child is not dry during the day.

MAINTAINING HEALTH

Children are susceptible to a range of illnesses, not all of which can be prevented, and they are accident-prone. Being aware of changes in your toddler's appearance and behaviour can alert you to problems early on, while safeguarding your home can go a long way to preventing dangerous situations, as can teaching your toddler about them as soon as he can understand.

HEALTH CHECKS

Toddlers come into contact with many other children and wider environments than when they were babies and are therefore exposed to more risks of illness. Sometimes, too, problems may appear in the toddler years which may not have been apparent in the first year. For instance, if your child is late in talking, this could indicate a hearing problem. You can help ensure that your child is growing up as healthy as possible by monitoring his well-being and developmental progress, and by taking some preventive measures.

The early detection of problems such as a vision defect or a hearing impairment can ensure the condition is treated successfully as soon as possible, and immunisations can prevent some serious or life-threatening diseases.

Just as importantly, many health problems can be forestalled or eased by good nutrition (see page 6), and attention to hygiene (see page 12) can ensure that your toddler does not suffer unnecessarily from some infections.

HEALTH CHECKS OR REVIEWS

It is important to take your toddler to the child health clinic or to your doctor for regular reviews. Your child may not always be given a full physical examination, but his general development will be assessed and you will be given the opportunity to discuss with your health professional any concerns that you may have about his growth, hearing or vision, any illnesses and sleep or behavioural problems he is experiencing.

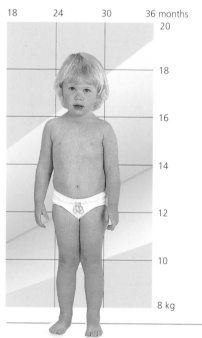

18	24	30	36 months

20

18

16

14

12

10

8 kg

GIRLS' AND BOYS' WEIGHT
In their early years, children are usually weighed at each check-up to ensure that they are growing at the correct rate for their age and gender. On the charts shown here, 50 per cent of children will fall above and 50 per cent below the middle line, while the upper and lower lines show the extremes. If your toddler falls outside of these, consult your doctor as weight problems in childhood may cause ill health in adulthood.

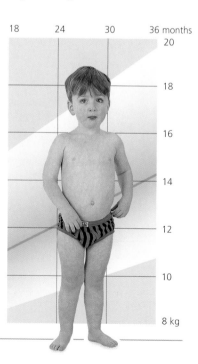

18	24	30	36 months

20

18

16

14

12

10

8 kg

IMMUNISATION SCHEDULE UP TO AGE FIVE

TWO TO FOUR MONTHS

★ **Polio** by mouth
★ **Hib, diphtheria, tetanus, whooping cough**
  one injection

12–15 MONTHS

★ **Measles, mumps, rubella (German measles)**
  one injection

THREE TO FIVE YEARS

★ **Measles, mumps, rubella**
  one injection (booster)
★ **Diptheria, tetanus**
  one injection (booster)
★ **Polio** by mouth (booster)

Toddlers usually have a health review between 18 months and two years, and between three and four years. At each review your health visitor or doctor will discuss with you what your child can do and may ask your child to perform some simple tests to check his motor ability, hand-eye coordination, language progress and understanding, social behaviour and overall health.

Your health visitor will assess your child's progress for his age, but bear in mind that every child's progress is individual. And, if your child is shy, he may not do what the health visitor asks him. Therefore, make sure that you tell the health visitor whether your toddler has performed that task at home.

IMMUNISATIONS

Also called vaccination or inoculation, immunisation is a way of giving your child

*AN UNPLEASANT EXPERIENCE
Your child may get upset by the experience of being injected and will need all your love and support.*

protection against a number of dangerous diseases. Although some of these diseases are rare, your child still needs to be protected.

When your child is immunised he is given a vaccine made up of a tiny amount of the bacteria or virus that causes the disease. These stimulate the body into producing antibodies against it.

Your child will be vaccinated at various times during his first five years. The Hib vaccine refers to Haemophilus influenzae type b. The measles, mumps and rubella shot is known as the MMR. Because the MMR does not always work well enough the first time (at 12–15 months) it is repeated again when your child is between the ages of three and five. Your child will also need boosters of other vaccines before he starts school (see above).

There are very few reasons why a child cannot be immunised, but your doctor will advise you if this is the case for your child.

Some children do have reactions to these shots, but serious complications are rare. The risk from the diseases are far greater than any risk from the vaccines.

*POLIO
Polio is usually given by mouth in the UK and the USA, although in some European countries it may be given by injection.*

CHECKING HEARING AND VISION

It is important that any hearing or sight problems that your child has are detected as soon as possible to avoid the development of further problems, such as delayed speech or hand-eye coordination. There are simple tests that you can carry out to check both hearing and vision.

TYPES OF HEARING LOSS

Conductive deafness This sort of deafness is usually temporary and treatable and occurs when sound is unable to pass through the ear drum and reach the middle or inner ear. It may happen because of a build up of ear wax or an object in the ear, or more commonly, a build up of fluid in the middle ear (glue ear, see page 45).

Sensorineural deafness Also called nerve deafness, this type of hearing loss is permanent and is most often caused by damage to the cochlea, the part of the ear that carries sound to the brain.

TESTING YOUR CHILD'S HEARING

You can carry out some simple hearing tests on your child. Make a game of these and don't let your child get anxious about them, or show him any anxiety if he does not respond.

Make sure the room is quiet, your child is in a cooperative mood and is not feeling too tired or hungry.

CHILD WATCH
Signs of hearing difficulty:
- Speech delay
- Indistinct or poor speech
- Lack of attention when someone is talking, especially if the speaker is behind the child
- Sitting very close to the television or radio or only hearing when the volume is turned up
- Repeated ear infections or is catarrhal
- Not turning when called
- Not liking listening to stories, especially in a noisy group
- Looking intently at a speaker's face
- Lacking confidence, unsure what to do or is uncooperative

18 months to two years When your child is distracted and the room is quiet, stand 90–180 cm (3–6 ft) behind him and make a high pitched sound, rustle some tissue paper or rattle something. Or ask him to identify different parts of his body, for example, 'show me your eyes'.

Two to three years
Sit 3 m (10 ft) away and ask him to put the toys in the bowl, one by one. Or, still at this distance and with your mouth covered, ask him in a quiet voice to point to his eyes, arms, feet, teeth, or to his shoes, socks, trousers, and so on.

If you have any doubts about your child's hearing after testing or at any time, always see your doctor without delay. He will either diagnose and treat the problem, or if necessary arrange for your child to be tested by an audiologist. Total deafness is rare, and there is a range of aids and treatments available for hearing problems.

QUICK HEARING CHECK
Sit your child at a low table with a bowl and some toys. Cover your mouth with a card. In a whisper ask him to identify the toys.

COMMON EYE PROBLEMS

Squints (Strabismus) The eyes do not look together in the same direction because the six muscles attached to the eyeball are not balanced correctly. Squints may run in families or follow an illness such as measles or chickenpox.

Long sight (Hypermetropia) This means your child sees distant objects better than near objects. The eyes may overfocus and develop a squint or double vision.

Short sight (Myopia) This causes a difficulty in seeing objects at a distance, but is uncommon in toddlers.

Astigmatism This causes distorted vision – it may occur in one eye only.

Lazy eye (Amblyopia) The eye does not work as well as it should and it may result in permanently impaired vision if left untreated. A lazy eye can be difficult to detect, so have your child's eyes tested regularly.

Colour blindness About 8 per cent of boys are colour blind compared to about 0.5 per cent of girls. The most usual form is being unable to distinguish red from green. You need to know if your child cannot distinguish certain colours for his own safety.

TESTING YOUR CHILD'S VISION

From the age of one your child should be able to see everything which an adult can see. Although you should make sure your toddler's vision has been professionally tested by the time he is three years, there are also some simple checks which you can do yourself.

To check near vision (18 months to three years) Ask your child to pick up a single 'hundred and thousand' or from the palm of your hand or from a table, or a crumb or cotton thread from the floor.

To check distant vision (two to three years)
Put one of two sets of small matching toys – such as a car, a child's knife, fork and spoon, a

small doll, a chair and a plane, on a table in front of your child. Walk 3 m (10 ft) away, hold up each toy and ask your child to show you the corresponding toy. From the age of three, repeat the test asking your child to cover one eye at a time. (It helps if you hold up the toys against a dark background.)

To check for a 'lazy eye' (two and a half to three years) Play a game of pirates using an eye patch made from a piece of cloth and elastic. Notice what eye he chooses to cover with the patch and what happens if you put the patch on the other eye. If he objects or strongly prefers one eye to the other, then have his vision checked. Treatment may involve covering the good eye to make the lazy eye work properly.

TO DETECT COLOUR BLINDNESS (TWO AND A HALF TO THREE YEARS) Put some bricks on the floor with two of each colour. Pick up a red one and ask your child to pick one the same colour. Repeat with other colours.

LOOKING AFTER A SICK CHILD

All children are ill at some stage of their lives, some more often than others. Fortunately, most illnesses are not serious and can be successfully treated at home. Parents usually know when their toddler is ill; he or she is generally off-colour, has a poor appetite, a raised temperature, and may be listless or irritable, complain of some pain, vomit or have loose stools. If your child has any of the following symptoms you should contact your doctor for advice:

★ **Temperature** If above 38°C (100°F) and below 35°C (95°F) (see also page 44).

★ **Vomiting** If intermittent during a six-hour period or if accompanied by fever or diarrhoea.

★ **Diarrhoea** If your child has loose watery stools for more than 48 hours or if they have blood in them (see also page 45).

★ **Pain** Headache after a head injury or bump particularly if accompanied by blurred vision, nausea or dizziness and abdominal pain, especially on the lower right side.

★ **Laboured breathing** If with sharp intake of ribs after a breath or if your child's lips are blue.

★ **Loss of appetite** Particularly if your child refuses food for 24 hours and seems lethargic.

NURSING YOUR CHILD

An ill child may be more demanding and irritable than usual, so you will need to be patient. Expect him to be more babyish than usual and to need help with things he would normally do himself. You may find this quite tiring so make sure you get a break occasionally.

Unless your doctor advises otherwise, or your child wants to go to bed, let him rest on a settee or armchair where he can be near you, and see what's going on. Keep the room your child is in warm but not too hot. Dress him in light, loose, comfortable clothes. Ventilate the room, but prevent draughts.

It is important to encourage your child to drink plenty of fluids. If he is reluctant to do so, offer him his favourite drink with colourful straws or in a special glass or cup. Freeze diluted juice into ice cubes which he can suck. He might find it comforting if you put his drink in a beaker or bottle, even if he has long outgrown them.

Offer him small amounts of light foods. Don't worry if he doesn't eat very much, as drinking is more important when he is ill.

Once your child is on the road to recovery but still not well enough to run around, you will also need to think up some entertainment to stop him getting bored. Besides reading him extra stories and giving him extra toys to play with you might wish to provide:

★ A cassette player and some tapes of your child's favourite nursery rhymes or stories.

★ Materials and toys for quiet play, such as jigsaws, colouring-in books and crayons, modelling dough and building bricks.

★ Dolls or teddies with which he can play doctors and nurses.

COMFORTING PLAY
Nursing a 'sick' teddy may help your child to feel better about his own illness.

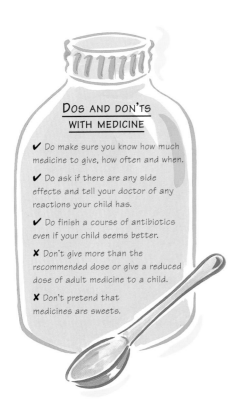

TAKING A TEMPERATURE

Under the age of five, you should not take your child's temperature by mouth as it is hard to get an accurate reading. Use a mercury or battery-operated digital thermometer under his arm. Sit your child on your knee and place the thermometer against the skin under his armpit. Hold your child's arm against his body and leave the thermometer in place for four or five minutes. If your child is restless, read him a story while doing this.

VOMITING

While your toddler is vomiting, hold him to reassure and comfort him. Make sure there is a bowl nearby for him to be sick into. Sit him on your lap and place one hand on his forehead to support his head, with the other over his stomach.

After he has vomited, reassure him and sponge his face to cool him down. Let him rinse his mouth out or help him brush his teeth to get rid of the unpleasant taste. Keep the bowl by the bed in case he vomits again.

GIVING MEDICINES

If your child needs to take medicine, have his favourite drink nearby to help take the taste away or tell him to hold his nose. If he is old enough to understand, explain that it will help him feel better. Use a 5 ml spoon or a liquid medicine measure and if he dislikes the taste, pour it onto the back of his tongue where it won't taste so strong. Always explain to your child what you are going to do. If your child cannot be persuaded at all, find out if the medicine is available in another form or flavour.

Inserting eye drops or ointment Wash your hands and then wash your child's eyes with cotton wool and lukewarm water. Lay your child on his back with his head in your lap. Cradle your arm around his head with your palm against his cheek. Tilt his head and gently draw his eyelids apart with your finger and thumb. If necessary ask someone to hold your child's head. Squeeze out the prescribed number of drops, or insert the ointment into the corner of the eye, being careful not to touch the eye. Keep your child still for a couple of minutes and repeat with the other eye.

Inserting ear drops Children often object to a cold substance being placed in the ear. If your doctor says you can warm it up, place the bottle of medication in a bowl of warm water. Test the temperature on the inside of your wrists before using it. Lay your child on a firm surface, with the ear to be treated facing you. Put in the prescribed drops. Wait a minute or two before repeating with the other ear.

Inserting nose drops If your child is old enough, encourage him to blow his nose first. Lay him on a firm surface with a pillow beneath his shoulders and his head tilted back. Put in the required number of drops and ask him to take a deep breath through his nose, or wait a minute or two before repeating with the other nostril. If necessary, ask someone to hold his head.

INSERTING EYE DROPS
You will need to hold your child's head firmly to ensure that the eye drops go in properly. Talk to him and distract him as you put the drops in.

HOSPITAL VISITS

If your child needs hospital treatment it is important to stay as calm as you can, as your toddler may pick up on your anxiety and become anxious or frightened.

As far as possible, try to prepare your child by playing doctors and nurses and by reading him books with hospital stories. Some hospitals also organise informal visits before admission.

Tell him that going into hospital will help make him feel better, and explain very simply what's going to happen. Answer any questions he may have in a simple but factual way. However, young children have little idea of time, so if you tell your child he is going into hospital he may expect to go immediately. Admittance may also be delayed, so a day or two before is best for a toddler. Tell your child that he will be coming home, but don't promise an actual day.

HELPING YOUR CHILD IN HOSPITAL

Try to stay with your child in hospital. If this is not possible, then being there for bed- and waking-up times and any procedures are the most important – but don't promise to be there at a particular time if you are not sure that you will make it.

Tell the nurse about personal things he or she needs to know about your child, such as if your toddler has a special word for the potty, if there is any particular food and drink he likes or dislikes, or if he has any particular habits, routines or comfort needs, such as a particular toy.

Soothe, calm and distract your child while procedures such as injections are being carried out. If you know or suspect something is 'wrong' with your child, tell the nurses. If you still do not feel reassured, ask to speak to your child's doctor.

Ask if you can participate in your child's care by giving him his medicine or bathing him.

Be truthful to your child as he will handle things better – he is likely to feel let-down and mistrustful if he is told that a certain procedure will not hurt and it does.

HAVING AN OPERATION

If it is necessary for your child to have surgery, again it will help to explain what is going to happen in as truthful and simple a way as possible. Play down any fears you may have, to prevent your child becoming overly anxious. You

WHAT TO PACK FOR YOUR CHILD

- Day and night clothes
- Washbag: soap, flannel, toothbrush, toothpaste, comb, hairbrush, towel
- Your child's favourite toy, books and comforter
- Games that don't require much concentration
- His own cup and beaker

should not hesitate to ask the doctor anything you are unsure of, for example, how the anaesthetic will be given and whether you will be allowed to stay with your child while it is given to him. It is very important that you try and be with him when he wakes up after an operation, since he may be frightened and your presence will be reassuring.

Warn your child in advance that he won't be able to eat or drink anything on the day of his operation. Tell him he will wear special clothes for the operation and a bracelet with his name on it. If he has stitches explain what they are and why he needs them and discourage him from scratching or playing with them.

HOME AGAIN

After a stay in hospital you may find that your child is difficult to manage at first. A younger toddler may be clingy and an older child may revert to babyish ways such as wanting a previously discarded comforter or wanting to be dressed. His toilet training may also be set back or regress completely. Be patient and reassuring – these are all normal reactions and will usually soon pass.

COMMON COMPLAINTS

ASTHMA

A steadily increasing complaint in children, asthma may be triggered by an allergy such as to the house dust mite, grass and tree pollens and animals. Other trigger factors include a respiratory infection, cigarette smoke or petrol fumes.

Symptoms A frequent cough, attacks of wheezing and breathlessness, colds which don't clear up.

Treatment If you suspect that your child has asthma, see your doctor. Drugs may be prescribed or your child may be referred to a special asthma clinic.

SIGNS OF ASTHMA
Wheezing brought on by exercise is often a sign that your child has asthma, and you should take him for a check-up.

COLDS AND COUGHS

Colds are caused by different viruses and your child is likely to get about eight colds a year until age 12, after which immunity builds up.

Symptoms A cough may develop with a cold but if your child is eating and breathing normally and there is no wheezing, usually it is nothing to worry about.

Treatment Although colds and coughs can cause discomfort they rarely need treatment. Antibiotics are not usually prescribed unless a chest infection develops. Apply petroleum jelly around your child's nose to stop it getting sore. Keep your child cool and give him plenty of fluids. Avoid overusing cough mixture – a warm drink of lemon and honey can be just as soothing.

Consult your doctor if your child seems to be having breathing difficulties or is wheezing, has a high temperature or seems to be in pain when coughing, or the cough continues for a long time.

RELIEVING COUGHS
Medicines should be used sparingly and on the advice of a doctor.

CROUP

A respiratory infection of the larynx or voice box, croup is caused by a virus or by bacteria. It is common in children up to the age of four.

Symptoms A harsh or barking cough, a runny nose, hoarseness, noisy breathing and fever.

Treatment Most cases of croup are mild and do not last long. If your child gets croup it can be very alarming, but stay calm or you may frighten him more. Reassure your child and sit him up. Give plenty of warm drinks and the recommended dose of paracetamol for any fever.

A steamy atmosphere may help breathing. This can be produced by boiling a kettle, running the hot taps in the bathroom, using a room humidifier or putting wet towels over the radiator. If using steam, take care to avoid scalding. Keep the door and windows closed and encourage your child to inhale.

Call your doctor immediately or take your child to hospital if your child becomes distressed, or has difficulty in breathing or swallowing, turns blue, or there is indrawing of the ribs or below the ribs, when breathing.

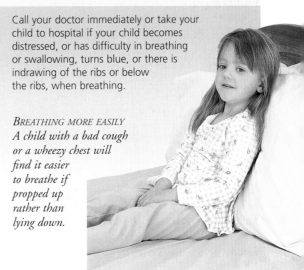

BREATHING MORE EASILY
A child with a bad cough or a wheezy chest will find it easier to breathe if propped up rather than lying down.

FEBRILE CONVULSIONS (FEVERISH FITS)

The normal body temperature is 37°C (98.6°F). If your child's temperature rises too far above normal (38.5°C or 101°F) this may result in febrile convulsions.

These are quite common, especially in children between the ages of six months and three years. They occur when the temperature rises too quickly for the child's immature temperature-lowering mechanism in the brain to cope.

Symptoms Your child suddenly becomes rigid, stares without blinking or his limbs start to twitch or jerk. He may become blue and lose consciousness for a few minutes.

Treatment To prevent a fever becoming convulsive:

Take his clothes off and sponge him down all over with tepid water. The evaporating water will help lower the temperature. Do not use cold water as this causes the blood vessels to contract and less heat will be lost.

Pat him dry and cover him lightly in a cotton sheet. Keep checking his temperature and gradually add clothes. If his temperature begins to rise again, repeat the sponging process or fan him. Give him plenty of cool drinks.

Dose him with paracetamol or ibuprofen according to your child's age and instructions on the packet. Never give asprin to a child under 12 unless directed to do so by a doctor.

COOLING A FEVER
Keep a feverish child cool by sponging him with tepid water. Cover him only with a cotton sheet, if at all.

If your child does develop convulsions, try not to panic, although they can be frightening. Follow the sponging procedure and make sure your child is cool but not chilly. Then do the following:

Move any objects that could be harmful out of the way and lie your child down on his tummy or side, with the head turned to one side and tilted back slightly, so that the airway is clear.

Remove any objects from your child's mouth. Do not put anything in the mouth.

Stay with your child. Most fits will stop after three minutes. Reassure your child and call your doctor or an ambulance.

ECZEMA

Atopic eczema is thought to affect one in eight children. The causes are not always known but include house dust, pets, pollen and sometimes foods such as cow's milk and eggs. However, food elimination diets should not be undertaken without professional advice from a doctor or a dietitian.

Atopic eczema tends to run in families and is associated with a family history of asthma or hayfever.

Symptoms Eczema usually starts with patches of dry, irritable, itchy skin on the face, behind the ears and knees, and in the folds of the neck and elbows. The skin may become red and inflamed with tiny pimples or blisters which can erupt into weeping or sore patches or may crack or scale.

Treatment It is essential to keep the skin soft and moist with the application of emollients or moisturising creams, several times daily. Suitable oils added to your child's bath may help. Use soap substitutes or emulsifying creams instead of soap.

Make sure your child does not dehydrate as this dries out the skin further. Always give him plenty of water to drink.

Sometimes steroid creams will be prescribed by your doctor to help the healing of badly damaged skin, and to keep the eczema at bay. Other treatments include medicated bandages and wet wraps. Finding out which treatment works best for your child may need patience.

If you suspect that your child's eczema is related to his diet consult a dietitian or naturopath.

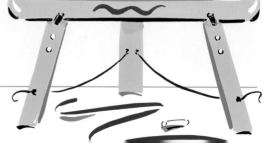

DOS AND DON'TS WITH ECZEMA

✔ Do try to identify and remove the cause.

✔ Do buy cotton clothing.

✔ Do damp dust and vacuum when your child is out of the room.

✔ Do use cotton or anti-allergy bedding.

✗ Don't use biological or perfumed detergents to wash your child's clothes. Rinse clothes thoroughly.

✗ Don't overheat your home as it will dry the air out.

EARACHE

A pain in the ear may be caused by an infection in the middle ear (*otitis media*), by another infection such as measles or mumps, or by toothache.
Symptoms Fever, severe pain, general unwellness, vomiting. If the ear drum bursts, yellow or green pus or blood may be seen in the ear or on the pillow.
Treatment If your child has earache but is otherwise well, give paracetamol for 12–24 hours. Do not put any oil or eardrops into your child's ear. If your child appears to have an infection, consult your doctor. Your doctor may either prescribe antibiotics or recommend paracetamol and decongestant nose drops.

RELIEVING EARACHE
A covered hot water bottle or a heat pad can be placed under your child's ear to relieve pain. After an ear infection your child may have a hearing problem for up to six weeks. If this persists see your doctor for advice.

GLUE EAR

Frequent bouts of *otitis media* may lead to glue ear, the most common cause of hearing difficulties in toddlers as it can prevent the sound waves vibrating through the ear to the hearing area of the brain.
Symptoms Partial hearing loss, a feeling of fullness in the ear, possible behavioural and speech problems.

Treatment Consult your doctor immediately. Treatment can include decongestant medicines and antibiotics, or surgery to open the ear drum (under general anaesthetic) and drain the fluid. Grommets (plastic ventilation tubes) are inserted to drain any remaining fluid from the middle ear. The adenoids may also be removed to prevent further blockage.

CONSTIPATION

Your child does not have to open his bowels every day, as long as his stools are soft and he does not appear to be in pain when he passes them.
Symptoms Long or irregular gaps before your child opens his bowels, accompanied by pain, abdominal discomfort and the passing of hard dry stools.
Treatment Give your child plenty of water to drink and fibre-rich foods such as fruits and vegetables, wholemeal bread and cereals to eat. Your child may become constipated if he dislikes or is afraid to sit on the toilet. If this is the case, let him go back to using his potty until he is ready to use the toilet.

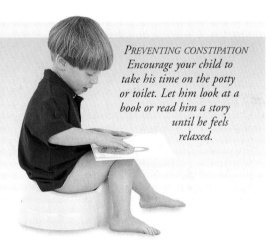

PREVENTING CONSTIPATION
Encourage your child to take his time on the potty or toilet. Let him look at a book or read him a story until he feels relaxed.

DIARRHOEA

Diarrhoea is usually caused by the rotovirus infection.
Symptoms Frequent, loose, watery, foul-smelling stools which may contain mucus and which may be brown, yellow or green. Young children may also get a condition called toddler diarrhoea where bouts of passing very loose stools, which may contain bits of undigested food, occur for no apparent reason.

Contact your doctor immediately if your child is also vomiting, the diarrhoea is very watery or has blood in it, the diarrhoea continues for more than 48 hours, or if your child has signs of dehydration (dry skin or mouth, sunken eyes, does not pass water for six to eight hours, or is listless).

Treatment Give your child plenty of clear fluids or an oral electrolyte fluid. Let him continue to eat if he wants to but avoid too much milk or fruit.

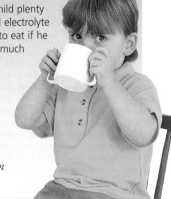

AVOID DEHYDRATION
It is important to rehydrate a child with diarrhoea – electrolyte fluids are available from pharmacies.

HEAD LICE

Most children catch head lice at some stage in their childhood, and it is no reflection on a family's standards of hygiene. Although lice are more common in schoolchildren, a young toddler can catch them, especially if she attends nursery or play group or has an older brother or sister who attends school.

Lice are tiny insects, slightly smaller than a match head. They live on hair near the scalp and can be difficult to see. They are only caught through close head-to-head contact and cannot jump or fly. **Symptoms** Contrary to popular belief, head itching is not the first sign of lice – they have usually been on the scalp for three or four months. Other signs include a rash on the scalp and lice droppings. These are black and powdery, like fine pepper, and may be seen on pillowcases.

The lice lay eggs which hatch after about 7–10 days. Nits are the empty eggshells which are white and may be found further down the scalp.

Detecting lice: If you think your child has lice, wet her hair and part it into about 30 sections. Comb each section thoroughly with a fine-tooth plastic nit comb over a sheet of white paper, or when your child is in the bath. Lice, usually grey or brown in colour, may be seen on the scalp or comb, or may fall on the paper or in the water. If you find lice on your child's head the whole family and close contacts should be treated.

Treatment Lice may be removed by wet combing or by insecticide preparations. Wet combing involves washing your child's hair in the normal way with shampoo. Apply lots of conditioner and comb through the hair from the roots while it is very wet with a fine-tooth comb. Wipe the comb between each stroke. Repeat this routine every three days for two weeks so that any lice which are still emerging from the eggs can be removed before they too lay eggs.

*REMOVING NITS
Combing the hair
for lice and nits
must be done
with a very fine-
toothed nit comb,
available from
pharmacies.*

THREADWORMS

Threadworms are very common in children. They are caught when the tiny eggs are picked up from hand contact or dirt or from under the nails and then passed to the mouth when your child sucks his fingers or eats. The eggs are then hatched inside the body and the worms travel down to the rectum, and lay their eggs around the anus, usually at night.
Symptoms Intense itching, sleep disturbance and abdominal pain. Suspect threadworms if your child who was previously dry at night starts to wet again for no apparent reason.

Threadworms can be seen as tiny white strands like cotton, around the anus or in the potty.
Treatment The whole family will need to take a threadworm medication. Your doctor or pharmacist can advise you on the appropriate product and dose.

Your child should wear pyjamas or pants in bed to stop him scratching his bottom and transferring the eggs back under his fingernails.

Bath your child or wash around his bottom each morning. Keep your child's towel separate.

Make sure everyone in the family washes their hands and scrubs their nails thoroughly before every meal and after going to the toilet to avoid reinfection.

Wash towels, clothing and bed linen in very hot water and tumble dry or dry over radiators or in strong sunlight to kill the eggs.

As eggs may be transmitted to surfaces such as taps, toilet seats and handles, disinfect these daily until the infection has passed. Also make sure you vacuum carpets thoroughly and dust in the bedrooms.

*PREVENTING INFECTIONS
Keep nails short to prevent your
child getting worm eggs (from dirt)
underneath them and to minimise the
risk of transferring these to the mouth.*

Infectious conditions

CHICKENPOX

A common and mild viral infection which most children have had by the age of ten. The virus is easily spread by airborne droplets. In rare cases it can lead to encephalitis.

Symptoms Spots appear mainly in crops over three to four days. These change to blisters and crust over. Your child has a slight fever and appears unwell and may have a headache.

Treatment Contact your doctor. Give paracetamol for a fever and plenty to drink. Never give aspirin as this can cause complications. To soothe the itching, apply calamine lotion, or give the child a tepid bath with a cup of bicarbonate of soda or oatmeal added. Your doctor may prescribe antiseptic cream.

Discourage scratching as it can cause scarring.

Try to keep your child away from anyone who is pregnant as contacting chickenpox in pregnancy may cause serious problems for the mother and baby. If your child was with anyone pregnant just before he became unwell, tell the woman to see her doctor.

CHICKENPOX
Spots are dark red and extremely itchy and form blisters.

FIFTH DISEASE (SLAPPED CHEEK SYNDROME)

A fairly common but mild viral infection, usually occurring in the spring.

Symptoms Slap mark on cheek which lasts one to two days. Over the next two to three days, a lacy red rash appears on the body. It may come and go for up to two weeks. There may be fever and nasal discharge.

Treatment Keep your child cool and give him plenty to drink. The child is not contagious once the rash appears so does not need to be kept away from others.

The rash generally causes no discomfort and goes away eventually without treatment. There are no complications.

GERMAN MEASLES (RUBELLA)

A viral disease which is usually mild in children but can be serious for adults, therefore it is best to be exposed to it as a child. Rubella can be prevented by immunisation.

Symptoms May start like a cold. Spots appear on the face, and spread to the rest of the body. The rash usually only lasts for a few days. Your child will usually feel fine but he may have a slight fever and enlarged lymph nodes at the back of his neck on the lower part of the skull.

Treatment Give him plenty to drink. Keep the child away from pregnant women – if a pregnant woman catches rubella during the first four months of pregnancy, there is a serious risk of damage to her baby.

FIFTH DISEASE
Hot red marks which look like a slap appear on the cheeks.

GERMAN MEASLES
Spots are bright red and appear first on the face.

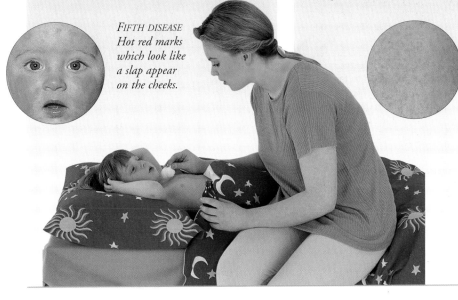

MEASLES

A highly infectious and potentially serious viral illness. Complications can include middle ear infection, croup, eye infections, convulsions, deafness and, rarely, brain damage or death. Measles can be prevented by MMR immunisation.

Symptoms Beginning with a runny nose, cough, headache and red, watery, sore eyes, your child then becomes more unwell with a high temperature. About three days after he first gets ill, a blotchy rash starts behind the ears and spreads to the face, trunk and limbs.

Treatment Call your doctor. Give your child plenty to drink and keep him cool. Give paracetamol to lower a temperature. Bathe the eyes with warm water. Antibiotics may be prescribed by your doctor to treat secondary infections, especially of the ears and lungs. Keep your child away from other children.

MUMPS

A mild viral illness with possible complications of meningitis, encephalitis and pancreatitis. Mumps can be prevented by the MMR immunisation. In children there is no risk of orchitis (inflammation of the testicles) and it is also very rare in adults with mumps.

Symptoms Your child may be unwell with a fever, headache, stiff neck and complain of pain around the ear and difficulty in swallowing, before a swelling appears below the ears or in front of the jaw. The swelling may be on one or both sides. He may also have a dry mouth and, less commonly, painful testicles and swollen ovaries.

Treatment If your child seems ill, call the doctor. Otherwise, keep him cool and give him paracetamol for the pain, and plenty to drink. Keep him away from other children. Observe for any signs of meningitis and call your doctor if you are concerned.

ROSEOLA INFANTUM (INFANT MEASLES)

A common but mild viral disease.

Symptoms A rose-pink rash which follows a three day slight or high fever in children, usually between six months and two years. The rash fades within 24 hours.

Treatment The high fever may cause convulsions. Keep your child cool – sponge him down with tepid water. Give him plenty to drink. Your doctor may prescribe medication. There are no complications from this illness.

MENINGOCOCCAL MENINGITIS

There are two types of meningitis – viral meningitis and bacterial meningitis. Hib meningitis was the most common bacterial form in children, but is now very rare because of Hib vaccine. However, Hib does not protect against other forms of bacterial meningitis such as menin-gococcal meningitis which is quite rare, but can be very serious. Menin-gococci bacteria is found in the nose and throat of people who are well. Only some people who carry the germs will develop meningitis. Children under five are more likely to be affected than adults because they have less natural immunity.

Symptoms Vomiting, headache/fever, neck stiffness, joint pains, drowsiness or confusion, dislike of bright lights, rash of red/purple spots or bruises that does not fade when pressed. The symptoms may not all be present at the same time. The disease can also cause septicaemia (blood poisoning).

A rash appears under the skin which starts as a cluster of tiny blood spots, which look like pin pricks. If untreated they get bigger, and look like fresh bruises. They can appear anywhere on the skin. The meningitis rash does not fade or turn white under pressure, whereas almost all other rashes do.

Treatment Contact your doctor urgently if your child becomes ill with one or more of these symptoms. Hospitalisation and intravenous antibiotics are necessary.

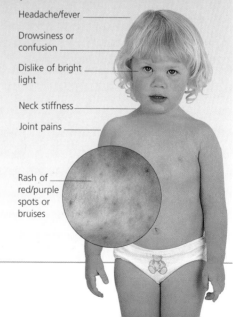

Headache/fever

Drowsiness or confusion

Dislike of bright light

Neck stiffness

Joint pains

Rash of red/purple spots or bruises

CALL YOUR DOCTOR IMMEDIATELY IF YOUR CHILD HAS A RED OR PURPLE RASH WHICH DOES NOT FADE WHEN THE SIDE OF A GLASS TUMBLER IS PRESSED AGAINST IT.

WHOOPING COUGH (PERTUSSIS)

Whooping cough is a very distressing disease and can be dangerous in young children. Complications can include pneumonia, convulsions, ear infections, brain damage and even death. It can be prevented by immunisation. Keep a child with whooping cough away from non-immunised babies.

Symptoms Starts with a cold and cough. The cough gradually gets worse and changes so that several bouts occur in succession. These are exhausting for your child who may find it difficult to breathe and may vomit or choke. The coughing usually, but not always, ends with a 'whoop' as the child gasps for breath. It may last for several weeks.

Treatment Call your doctor. Antibiotics will be needed, and in severe cases, hospitalisation. Keep your child cool. Give drinks and offer food immediately after a coughing bout.

WHOOPING COUGH
If your child is having a choking coughing fit, place him on your knee, lean him forward and gently pat and rub his back to help loosen the mucus.

IMPETIGO

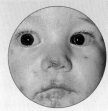

IMPETIGO
Small red spots form which then fill with fluid.

This common bacterial skin infection in children usually occurs around the nose and mouth. It spreads rapidly, especially in warm weather. Complications can include swelling of lymph nodes, septicaemia or kidney inflammation.

Symptoms Spots form blisters filled with yellow sticky fluid which oozes from the skin. The fluid dries to form honey-coloured crusts on the skin.

Treatment Consult your doctor immediately as impetigo spreads rapidly if left untreated. Topical antibiotics, covered by dressings, and sometimes oral antibiotics will be needed. Use warm water to wash away crusted areas and pat dry with paper towels. Keep your child's flannel, towels and bedlinen separate from the rest of the family. Keep your child at home until he is fully recovered.

RINGWORM

Ringworm is caused by a fungus, not worms. It may cause bald patches on the scalp.

Symptoms Itchy round patches on scalp or trunk.

Treatment See your doctor. Minor infections are treated with an anti-fungal cream, but severe infections or those involving the nails and scalp may also need oral antifungal tablets. As ringworm is infectious, keep the pillows, towels and combs of the infected child separate from those of the rest of the family.

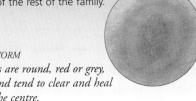

RINGWORM
Patches are round, red or grey, scaly and tend to clear and heal from the centre.

SCABIES

SCABIES
The tiny red dots caused by scabies are intensely itchy at night.

Caused by a microscopic mite that burrows into the skin and lays eggs.

Symptoms Itchy, scattered red dots between the fingers and toes, and around the wrist, ankle, penis, and waist. Also seen as a dark spot at the tip of their grey, scaly burrowing trails.

Treatment It is highly contagious so the whole family must be treated. Apply a scabicide lotion (ask your doctor or pharmacist about the best one for your child and the family). Wash all clothes and bedlinen to prevent reinfection as mites can live independently of human skin for up to six days.

SAFETY AT HOME

Accidents both outside and inside the home are the commonest cause of death and injury among children over the age of one. Therefore it is vital to protect your toddler from danger, while not stifling his natural curiosity and growing independence.

Some accidents may happen no matter your child's age – such as slipping on a rug on a polished floor; others depend on your toddler's level of development – your child would have to be at least two before he'd be able to unscrew bottles and drink the contents. While it is impossible to make your home completely accident proof, or to keep your eyes on your toddler 24 hours a day, you do need to stay one step ahead of your child by taking appropriate safety measures around your home. A child under the age of three cannot be expected to understand and remember everything you tell him about danger and safety. But as he grows and in line with his understanding, you can teach him about dangers and simple accident prevention.

KEEPING YOUR CHILD SAFE

Between the age of 15 months and two years, your child is likely to be walking confidently, climbing, and be 'into everything'. He will be

CURIOUS CLIMBER
Never leave anything dangerous, breakable or precious within reach of a toddler. Put tablecloths away as they will only help him to reach items.

DOS AND DON'TS WITH HOME SAFETY

✔ Do make your home as accident-proof as possible, without overprotecting your child.

✔ Do be aware that your child will copy your actions and always set him a good example.

✔ Do teach your child about danger as soon as he is old enough to understand.

✘ Don't ever leave your young child alone in the house or garden.

✘ Don't assume he will understand or obey you if you tell him something is dangerous.

opening your drawers and cupboards, be fascinated by water, and grabbing and pulling things such as leads on kettles, teapots on tables, and hanging tablecloths. Your child will have no sense of danger – and will be starting to copy many of your actions. If he sees you smoking a cigarette or drinking alcohol from a glass, for example, and these items are then left lying around, he may be tempted to eat or drink them.

From the age of 15–18 months your child can understand simple instructions and the meaning of the word 'no' if this is said in a firm voice. Be careful, however, not to overuse 'no'; saying it for every minor action your child does may result in him ignoring it when he is really in danger. Your child can also begin to learn the consequences of some actions – such as, if he touches something hot, it will hurt. You can hold his hand near a hot fire or cooker, or put it briefly on a warm kettle and tell him: 'it's hot, and if you touch it it will burn you.'

By the time your child reaches three he will understand and remember what danger means. You will then be able to start to teach him how to do or use things safely, however, you should never overestimate his understanding. He will lack the experience to estimate danger accurately, even if he seems mature for his age.

It is not always easy to steer a middle path, but overprotecting your child can be as dangerous as underprotection. If your child is not allowed to do anything on his own for fear that he will get hurt, he may become defiant and take unnecessary risks, or become nervous and be more likely to have an accident.

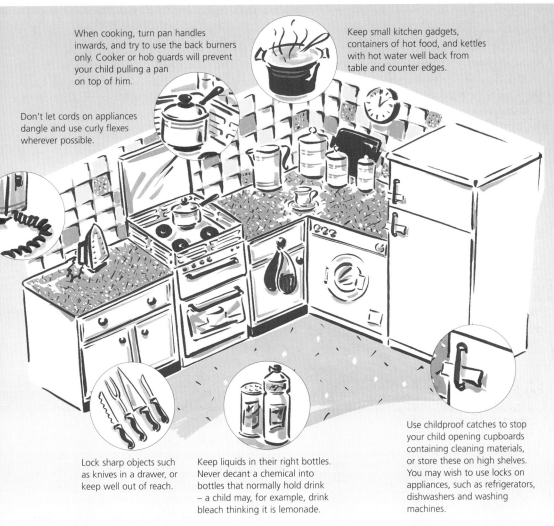

When cooking, turn pan handles inwards, and try to use the back burners only. Cooker or hob guards will prevent your child pulling a pan on top of him.

Keep small kitchen gadgets, containers of hot food, and kettles with hot water well back from table and counter edges.

Don't let cords on appliances dangle and use curly flexes wherever possible.

Lock sharp objects such as knives in a drawer, or keep well out of reach.

Keep liquids in their right bottles. Never decant a chemical into bottles that normally hold drink – a child may, for example, drink bleach thinking it is lemonade.

Use childproof catches to stop your child opening cupboards containing cleaning materials, or store these on high shelves. You may wish to use locks on appliances, such as refrigerators, dishwashers and washing machines.

ROOM-BY-ROOM SAFETY
Safety in the kitchen
Your child probably loves being in the kitchen with you, but it can be a dangerous place for a toddler. Potentially, it is the most lethal area of the home. Hot kettles, irons, cookers, knives and other sharp implements, cleaning agents and other chemical substances – it's impossible to remove all sources of danger, so you will need to

be extra careful about hazards here. Always supervise your child in the kitchen, regardless of his age, and teach him not touch anything without your permission.

In addition to the safety measures illustrated, you should have a fire extinguisher and fire safety blanket close to hand.

Sitting room

Potential dangers include poisonous plants, unstable and sharp cornered furniture, glass tables, low-level windows and open fires. If you have a video, you may wish to buy a lock to prevent your child stuffing things in it.

Bathroom

Always supervise your child in the bathroom and don't let him run his own bath. If a toilet is near a window, use a window lock. Store medicines, razors and cleaners where your child cannot climb to reach them. If your child is curious about what's in the toilet, you may need to fit a toilet seat lock. Make sure the bath and shower have slip resistant surfaces or a slip resistant mat. The bath should have a safety grip handle to help prevent falls (see also page 13).

Bedroom

Check for general safety measures in your child's bedroom, such as access to windows, electrical outlets and stairs. Secure any trailing wires which could trip your child up. A guard rail on the bed helps protect a restless sleeper. Don't let your young child sleep in a top bunk bed. If you have heavy doors or ones that slam easily, fit finger protectors.

PREVENTABLE DANGERS

A home contains many potential sources of accidents of which you need to be aware. Most accidents are preventable but toddlers, with their boundless curiosity and newfound agility, need a lot of protection.

Choking, strangulation and suffocation

As your child gets older choking becomes less of a danger but he can still gag on small objects such as food.

★ Until he is five, do not give your child boiled sweets or whole nuts; peanuts are especially dangerous as they can be inhaled, and contain aracis oil which can damage the lungs.

★ Be careful not to leave small objects around which your child could swallow. Take particular care with button batteries as they may contain mercury that

SAFETY EVERYWHERE
Children love to open closed doors so you need to make sure that every room in the house is safe for your toddler to venture into.

can leak if swallowed. If your child does swallow one, take him to your nearest accident and emergency department immediately.

★ Check toys do not have small detachable parts
★ Make sure there are no trailing wires or cords which he could wrap around his neck and don't let him wear clothes with draw strings around the neck.
★ Keep deflated balloons away from your child – he may suck these into his mouth and choke or suffocate. Polythene bags and plastic are similarly dangerous – keep these hidden away and teach him not to put them over his head.

Scalds and burns

Children's skin is thinner than an adult's, so they can get burnt or scalded at lower temperatures. Hot water can still scald for half an hour after it has boiled so don't leave hot drinks or dishes of hot food within reach of your child.

★ Keep your hot water temperature turned down to 54°C (130°F), to help prevent scalding. It is not a good idea to leave a hot water bottle in your child's bed as this could cause burns.
★ Keep a fixed fireguard in front of gas, electric or open fires, and in front of open or wood burning

stoves. Don't put mobile fires where they can be knocked over, or hang mirrors above fires.

★ Make sure your child's night-clothes are fire resistant and furniture is covered in fire retardant material.

★ Keep matches and cigarette lighters out of his reach.

★ Fit smoke detectors on the ceiling of every level of the house. Buy one which is made to approved safety standards and follow the manufacturer's instructions for fitting. Test the button regularly to make sure it is working and replace the battery when necessary, making sure this is at least once a year.

Drowning

Remember that a young child can drown in just a few inches of water.

★ Don't leave your toddler unattended in the bath, even for a few moments. If the telephone or doorbell rings, ignore it or take your child out of the bath before answering.

★ Don't leave buckets of water around – your child may fall into them and be unable to get out.

★ Always supervise your child if he's playing near water and fence off garden ponds or cover them until your child is older.

★ It is a good idea to teach your child to swim as early as possible.

Cuts and gashes

Low-level or fixed glass in and around doors and low cupboards can break or splinter if your child bumps into it, causing serious injuries. It is wise to replace it with safety glass or plywood. Or cover it with safety film – this will not stop the glass breaking but it will hold the shards together and reduce the risk of a serious accident.

Poisoning

★ Lock harmful products such as chemicals, medicines and cleaning materials away or put them where your child cannot climb to reach them. Remember, children are good climbers!

★ Don't leave tablets in your handbag or pockets and never refer to them as sweets. Keep medicines and other potentially harmful products in containers with child-resistant tops, but remember these are not childproof.

★ Put poisonous house plants well out of your child's reach and teach him not to eat or pick anything from the garden without asking you first.

Tumbles and falls

Windows should have fitted locks or catches to prevent your child opening them more than 10 cm (4 in). However, make sure that you are still able to open them easily in case there is a fire.

Windowsills should not be accessible for your child to climb on, nor should they provide a ledge to sit on. If you can, move furniture such as beds or chairs, so that they are not directly under the windows.

★ Floors should be non-slippery and scatter rugs should be avoided on polished floors. Try to wipe up any spills immediately.

★ Furniture should be stable and not tip over easily. Protectors should be fitted on sharp table corners. Put small objects and ornaments away until your child is older.

★ Safety gates will need to be fitted at the top and bottom of the stairs until your child confidently walks up and down without too much danger of him falling. Check that he cannot fall or squeeze through, crawl under, or climb over, banisters or landing rails. If necessary, block these up with hardboard or close netting.

Shocks and electrical burns

Modern electrical sockets are designed not to give a shock, but if these are old, or easily accessible, it is best to fit socket covers.

As your child may encounter uncovered sockets in other people's homes, you should in any case teach him not to put his fingers or any objects into sockets and tape down switches so that he can't turn them on.

Check too that you have no frayed electrical cords and that your wiring is not too old, as these can cause a fire.

Avoid buying electrical goods from second-hand shops or markets as you have no guarantee of their safety.

SAFETY OUTDOORS

As well as taking safety measures in your home, you will also need to make sure your child is safe when she plays outside, or when you visit other people's homes.

SAFETY IN THE SUN

Although children need some sun and fresh air to keep healthy, you need to protect your child from over-exposure to the sun, and from getting sunburnt. Not only is sunburn very painful for your child, but every sunburn increases her risk of getting skin cancer in later life. The fairer your child is, the greater the danger.

Keep your child out of the sun when it's at its strongest – this is usually between 11am and 3pm. Always protect her skin with a sunscreen. Use one especially formulated for children or one with a minimum sun protection factor (SPF) of 15, which is effective against the UVA and UVB rays of the sun. Reapply often, especially after swimming. Use a waterproof sunscreen while in the water.

Always encourage your child to play in the shade but watch out for surfaces such as snow, sand, water, concrete and glass which can reflect the sun's rays. Children can also get burnt on cloudy or overcast days so always apply sunscreen in the summer even on a dull day.

Don't let your child wear cheap sunglasses in the sun – you need to protect her eyes with sunglasses with an ultra-violet filter.

If your child does get sunburnt:
★ Cool her with a tepid bath, shower or cool compress. Apply calamine lotion or an after-sun cream. Don't burst any blisters. Give her cool drinks as she may be dehydrated, and a dose of paracetamol. Keep her indoors.

COVER UP FROM THE SUN
Dress your child in loose cotton clothing and a sunhat. Protect her shoulders and back of neck as these are vulnerable to sunburn.

★ If your child has severe sunburn, or is shivering, feverish or vomiting, see your doctor.

ROAD SAFETY

When you take your toddler out walking, use reins or hold her hand firmly to keep her securely by your side. If she is in a buggy, fasten her harness every time and take care not to overload it with shopping in case it tips over. Teach her road safety by your example: find a safe place to cross and explain why you have to stop, look and listen, before crossing the road. Teach your child to look out for the 'green man' and the 'red man' at pedestrian traffic lights. Don't let your child go near a road or cross on her own.

IN THE CAR

When taking your child out in the car, make sure you comply with the law regarding the use of child seats, restraints and where she sits in the car. Ensure your child's car seat is correctly fitted according to manufacturer's instructions. If in doubt, have it fitted professionally. Also, fitting child locks on the doors is a must.

Never let your child travel in any car, such as a friend's or hire car, without a suitable restraint. The likelihood of injury in an accident can be reduced by two-thirds if your child is securely strapped into the appropriate and correctly fitted car seat for her age.

Inflatable airbags fitted to the front seats of a car are very dangerous to young children. If they inflate they can suffocate or injure children. If your car is fitted with front seat airbags, then always fit your child's car seat to the rear seats.

Never leave your child alone in a car, even for a couple of minutes. She may get too hot and she may also feel anxious.

IN THE PLAYGROUND

Your child needs the freedom and experience of playing in parks or playgrounds as part of growing up, but again you will need to be aware of potential hazards, such as unsafe equipment, animal mess and ponds. Whenever possible, let her run around in a fenced off play area.

Check that the ground beneath play equipment is soft, and teach your child not to run in front of equipment such as swings and roundabouts.

Teach your child not to run up to or touch strange dogs without permission.

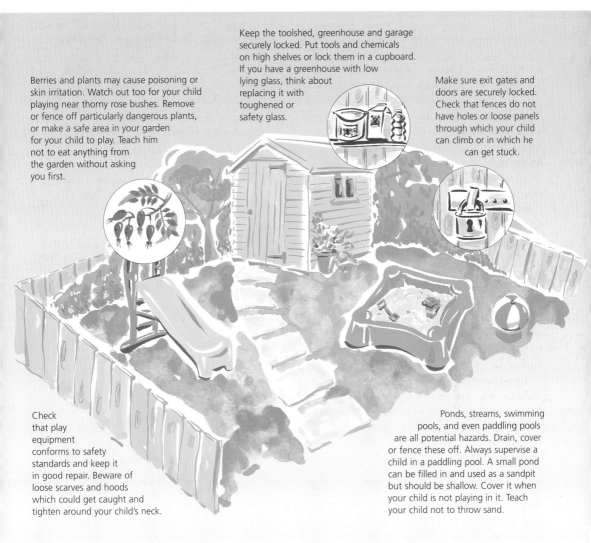

Berries and plants may cause poisoning or skin irritation. Watch out too for your child playing near thorny rose bushes. Remove or fence off particularly dangerous plants, or make a safe area in your garden for your child to play. Teach him not to eat anything from the garden without asking you first.

Keep the toolshed, greenhouse and garage securely locked. Put tools and chemicals on high shelves or lock them in a cupboard. If you have a greenhouse with low lying glass, think about replacing it with toughened or safety glass.

Make sure exit gates and doors are securely locked. Check that fences do not have holes or loose panels through which your child can climb or in which he can get stuck.

Check that play equipment conforms to safety standards and keep it in good repair. Beware of loose scarves and hoods which could get caught and tighten around your child's neck.

Ponds, streams, swimming pools, and even paddling pools are all potential hazards. Drain, cover or fence these off. Always supervise a child in a paddling pool. A small pond can be filled in and used as a sandpit but should be shallow. Cover it when your child is not playing in it. Teach your child not to throw sand.

IN THE GARDEN

Children love the freedom of exploring in the garden and they may love to help do your gardening too. But, like in your home, you will need to take safety precautions to ensure your child can play without the risk of an accident.

Keep children away when building bonfires or having barbecues; clean up any dog or cat faeces straight away; secure the lids of rubbish bins so that your child can't go rummaging and make sure all ladders are locked away so your toddler can't climb them. If your car is near the garden make sure your child is nowhere near it when it's moving or you are working on it.

PLAY AND ACTIVITIES

Play is a central part of your child's toddler years and has great educational value. It is important, however, that you oversee play, and join in as much as possible to ensure it promotes his physical and intellectual development. Try to strike a balance between structured and self-directed play; the latter will help him develop independence and a sense of his own identity.

THE IMPORTANCE OF PLAY

One of the most important ways in which your growing child learns to develop and practise his skills is through play. Not only does play provide mental, physical and social stimulation, but it also increases your child's powers of observation and concentration. Giving your child different types of toys and objects with which to play helps him to develop self expression, hand-eye coordination, and stimulates his creativity and imagination; they will also help him to learn to distinguish different shapes, colours, sizes, textures, sounds and weights. Play also helps to divert aggression, and helps your child to gain a sense of independence and to act out stressful situations by role play.

CHOOSING TOYS
There is a wide variety of toys on the market. The best ones to choose are not only those that are right for your child's age and abilities, but which can also be used in more than one way; these are the most likely to retain his interest. A pull-along telephone, for example, will not only teach him about sound and touch, it can also promote hand-eye coordination and stimulate his imagination. If a toy is too advanced for your child's age or developmental stage, he will quickly become frustrated and abandon it, or prefer to play with the box the toy came in! If a toy is too simple, he will soon become bored with it.

Your toddler needs variety in his toys and play equipment and homemade or inexpensive items can often provide much pleasure. A ball, or crayons and pieces of wallpaper to scribble on, can be as entertaining as more expensive items. The world in and around your child's home is also his playground, and simple indoor and outdoor activities are usually enjoyed by toddlers. There are also many household items with which he will enjoy playing.

With so many toys to choose from nowadays, you may find it difficult to decide which ones to buy. Expensive 'educational' toys will only be played with if your child finds them fun or interesting. Good buys are versatile toys which can be used to stimulate the imagination, and over a long period of time. Wooden building bricks, for example, will continue to be used by your child for several

PARENT PLAY
Your toddler doesn't always need a toy to play with – mums and dads are often much more fun.

years. Let your child play with a limited number of toys at a time – if he has too many to choose from he may run from one to another and keep changing his mind which one to play with. If he is given several toys for an occasion such as Christmas or his birthday, save a few for later and present one as a new toy on a rainy day, or when he is bored or not well.

15–18 months Your child will be curious about everything and trying to explore wherever he can; provide him with a large box of household items to tip out and rummage through and a selection of picture books in which he can point out recognisable items. He will also enjoy cardboard boxes and containers, simple puzzles, posting boxes, books, paper and crayons and miniature household objects such as a brush and dustpan.

Your child will also want to perfect his walking skills, so toys that require pushing and pulling will be helpful.

Two years As your child approaches his second birthday, his locomotive skills will become more advanced and he will enjoy kicking and throwing balls, building blocks, scribbling on paper, and imaginative play. Other favourites will be musical toys with nursery rhymes, hammer pegs, chatter telephones, tea sets, balls, sandpits and paddling pools (under supervision).

Three years Towards the age of three, your child will have much more finely controlled hand movements, and enjoy construction toys, doing simple jigsaws, threading large beads and looking at books. Playing with sand, water, dough and paint will encourage exploration, coordination and creativity. Suitable toys also include cotton reels for threading, dressing up clothes, sit-and-ride toys, swings, a bucket and spade.

Three and a half to four years By now your child will have considerably improved his locomotive skills, hand-eye coordination, and language and social skills. At this age, he can ride a tricycle or pedal car, and will enjoy climbing frames, which he uses with increased agility. Blunt-ended scissors to cut out pictures in magazines will encourage his manual dexterity and he will enjoy making collages. He will engage in make-believe and may have imaginary companions and objects. He will love playing at being an adult by himself or with his friends.

MUM'S LITTLE HELPER
Mixing a cake can provide far more entertainment than you think!

HELPING YOUR CHILD TO PLAY
A very important factor in your child's mental, physical and social development is your involvement in his play and activities. Young children find it hard to play alone for long. Indeed, if your toddler has sat playing quietly for more than a short time, you will probably suspect some mischief, and go to check up on him. Your child also will need you to help guide his play to some extent, to demonstrate how things work if necessary, and to encourage his efforts at activities such as drawing and making things.

When you cannot be available to play with your child, try to involve him in your daily activities – for example let him help you wash up, mix a cake or dust; not only will it be fun for him but he will have an opportunity to learn new skills and actions.

As your child gets older you will need to strike a balance between helping your child and leaving him free to play in the way he chooses. If you are constantly playing with him he will not learn to entertain himself and will become bored or miserable when on his own. And if you are constantly interfering with, or taking over, his play he will not learn how to do things for himself and gain self-confidence.

It is also a good idea to check his toys regularly. Are they still safe (see page 52)? Has he outgrown them? If your child has become bored with a toy, but it's still within his age range, put it away for a week or two and then bring it out again. He will probably welcome it as a new toy.

PLANNING ACTIVITIES

Your child's age, attention span and stage of development should determine your choice of activities. Each day try to include both active and passive play, both indoors and out, and try to meet up with other parents and children to give both yourself and your toddler the chance to socialise. Even though your child may not want to play directly with other children until he is about two and a

AVOIDING STEREOTYPES
Try not to be sexist when choosing toys – most boys love playing with dolls, and pushing doll's buggies, and most girls enjoy cars and construction toys as much as boys.

HOUSEHOLD ITEMS

Start a box containing 'junk' and household objects for your child to play with. Add to it as he grows. Include: wooden spoons, plastic cartons, empty cotton reels, pegs, magazines to tear up, saucepan lids to bang together, egg cartons, small plastic bottles, empty food boxes, clothes for dressing up.

half, he will enjoy playing alongside them. Later on he will enjoy going to a play group or nursery group, where he can join in a variety of activities with children his own age and practise his social skills.

Different types of play are important to avoid boredom and to challenge your child. Stimulate his physical development with running, climbing, jumping throwing a ball, riding a bike and dancing; encourage his creativity, imagination and expression through modelmaking, drawing and painting, dressing up, pretend tea parties and fantasy play; strengthen his hand-eye coordination with building blocks, construction toys, puzzles and shape sorters; and perfect his social skills by letting him play alongside or with other children.

As well as stimulation from various toys and activities, sometimes your child also needs to do nothing at all – and be allowed to sit and day dream, act out a fantasy in his mind or talk to imaginary friends, unwind and think about the day's events, or just have a quiet cuddle with you.

MESSY PLAY

Activities such as playing with water, sand, mud, playdough, splashing through puddles, cooking and painting, are extremely important for your child. They make use of the senses of touch, sight, sound, taste and smell and allow your child to explore and experiment with different materials.

If your child is afraid of making a mess or is never allowed to be dirty, this can inhibit his creative abilities and deter him from joining in these activities when he goes to playgroup or nursery school.

Rather than worrying about him getting dirty, cover your child up with an old shirt put on back to front, or with a waterproof apron or overall and set aside an area for messy play. If your child delights in getting dirty most of the time, try to accept it as part of growing up – he will grow out of it eventually.

OUT TO TEA
Between the ages of 18 months and two years your toddler will begin to enjoy make-believe play – a plastic tea set will provide the opportunity to pretend as well as to socialise.

PLAY SAFETY

When choosing toys for your child, it is essential to make sure that they are safe and comply with current safety regulations, where applicable. Look for the appropriate stamp or label.

Always supervise young children playing. This is very important when they are playing with older children as they may be tempted to play with toys that are not suitable.

Toy safety Take a toy out of its box and examine it carefully. Check that it is sturdy and well built, and that small parts such as wheels on cars, or eyes on soft toys, are secure. Consider whether it can be easily broken or if it has small parts that can be easily detached and swallowed. Are there any materials that could be toxic if chewed? Look for sharp edges or ridges which could cut your child. If it is big enough for your child to climb into, does it have adequate ventilation? If it contains water, is it adequately sealed? Avoid buying potentially dangerous toys second-hand or from market stalls.

Accidents can also be caused by a child falling over a toy, badly maintained toys, or lack of supervision. A small child may swallow a toy or insert a small part in an orifice. Batteries which leak may also cause an acid burn.

Although your child will enjoy dressing up in old clothes, take care that he does not trip up in overlong clothes, wear shoes with high heels which could cause a fall, and that there are no loose buttons on which he could choke.

Help to make his games as realistic as possible while keeping them safe – for instance he could 'make tea' with cold milk and water.

Safety outside Check slides, climbing frames and swings regularly for loose parts and look carefully at equipment in local playgrounds before deciding if it is safe for your child to use (see page 55).

Don't encourage your child to climb higher than he wants to on play equipment or let him show off by going higher than he is capable of. Teach him that if he gets stuck or scared on a piece of equipment, he must stay still, calm and call you.

Make sure his footwear and clothes are suitable for playing on equipment. There should be no strings on hoods that can get caught and shoes should be firm-fitting with a good grip and properly laced.

Make sure you teach your child about the potential dangers of playing with strange dogs or cats, particularly stray ones.

DOS AND DON'TS WITH TOYS

✔ Do examine toys such as bikes or climbing frames regularly for loose parts.

✔ Do discard broken toys immediately.

✘ Don't let your child change batteries, and ensure that battery compartments on toys are inaccessible.

✘ Don't let your child leave toys lying around where they can be tripped over.

✘ Don't ever let your child play unsupervised near, or with, water.

BOOKS AND READING

It is never too early to start introducing your child to books. Not only will she enjoy looking at the pictures, and listening to the stories, but also the one-to-one attention and closeness to you. Reading to your child will also help to develop her speech and vocabulary, teach her about colours and shapes, the names of objects, and how other people live. Simple stories, or pictures such as a child going shopping, can also help your child relate to her own experiences. Books will also stimulate her imagination, and encouraging a love of books will ultimately help your child learn to read.

LEARNING LETTERS
Buy magnetic letters which you stick on metal surfaces such as the refrigerator and help your child spell out her name with these. Spell out other simple words such as 'cat' and 'dog'. Let your child play with these and she will begin to connect them to language. Teach her the alphabet song, or the different alphabet sounds, and serve her alphabet soup. When you are out and about look for large signs such as 'stop' and spell out the individual letters followed by the word, to your child. As she gets older, simple ABC books will also help her to recognise letters, but don't push her to read until she is ready.

READING TO YOUR CHILD
Try to read to your child once or twice a day and at the same time, such as before she goes to bed. Make the atmosphere cosy. At first her attention span will be brief, so keep the stories short.

A young toddler is likely to try to grasp the pages. Under the age of two, she will turn them over a few pages at a time, but after this age she will be able to manage single pages. When you read to your child she is learning how a book

READING TOGETHER
Reading with your child is important for her development as well as providing an opportunity for you to be together.

works – that you start at the front pages, turn these over one at a time, read from left to right, start at the top of a page, finish at the back, and that a story has a beginning, middle and end.

As you read, trace your finger along the words, but don't force your child to follow the words and take care not to obscure the pictures. Point to the pictures as you speak; eventually she will realise that the words are linked with the pictures. Make the story sound interesting and alive by putting plenty of expression in your voice and making appropriate sounds. For instance, make animal noises if the story involves animals or train sounds if you are reading about trains. Once your child becomes familiar with a story, encourage her to make these noises herself.

As she gets older, you can break off in the middle of a familiar story and ask your child what happens next. Or, when reading a new story, you can ask your child if she can guess what happens next. Also, develop her observational skills with books like spot-the-difference.

Teach your child to take care of her books – explain that books for reading are not to be scribbled in or torn. A well thumbed book is an indication, however, of how much your child has enjoyed it. Let your child see you enjoying reading – she will probably want to copy you and do the same.

TYPES OF BOOKS
During the second year it is best to have two types of books for your child – thick board books

with clear bright pictures which will stand up to tough handling, and which your child can look at on her own, and books to show her and read to her. 'Lift the flap' and 'pop-up' books are a great favourite, as are books with different textures. Small picture books which show one object on a page such as a pair of shoes, or a car, can be pointed out to your child. By the age of 18 months she will usually be able to identify some of these herself. Your toddler will also enjoy looking at books that show her everyday experience, such as going to the shops or getting dressed, and books with nursery rhymes and jingles. Books with rhyming words are also essential for language development.

There are an immense range of books to choose for two to three-year-olds, and your child's attention span will be improving. To help her memory and concentration, choose picture books with lots of detail – spend time talking about them with her and asking her to point things out. She will also enjoy hearing new stories and old favourites, books featuring characters which she may have seen on television, simple fairy tales and counting books (by the age of three she may be able to count up to ten). By the age of three, your child's vocabulary will also have increased considerably and when reading books, you can encourage her to guess the storyline. Some words and letters will be familiar and she may be able to

BOOK LOADS OF FUN
Your child's love of books will provide him with endless hours of entertainment and learning opportunities.

write the first letter of her name. She will also enjoy being allowed to choose her own books.

TAPES AND VIDEOS
Many children's books are now available as stories on tapes and videos. Although not a substitute for looking at books or reading to your child, these can be an additional way for your child to enjoy books. Also buying your child books featuring her favourite television characters may stimulate an interest in reading. It is obviously more beneficial if you and your child can watch a video together or look at the book while listening to the tape. Don't, however, let videos become a replacement for looking at books. Tapes can be useful for your child to listen to on a long car journey.

MAKING YOUR CHILD HIS OWN BOOK
One way to encourage your child to love books is to help her to make her own. You can use a photo album, scrap book, notebook or glue white pieces of paper onto the pages of an old book. Glue a photo of your child on the cover and write her name on it. You can then illustrate the book with pictures of her favourite objects; leave pages blank for your child to colour or copy pictures, or write a story with her as the central character, using photos or pictures to illustrate her activities. Make this an ongoing and interactive project. Every few days you could ask her if she wants to write more of the story and she could tell you what exciting activities she has done lately that she would like to go in the book.

PAINTING AND DRAWING

Young children naturally want to draw from an early age – even drawing lines in the sand with fingers or a spade, or tracing lines through some spilt drink is a form of drawing. Painting and drawing is also an ideal way for your child to express herself. Provide a variety of colours and tell your child which one she is using. Use different types of paper such as scrap paper, wallpaper, computer paper, cardboard or drawing paper. You can make a blackboard by painting a sheet of plywood, hardboard or stiff cardboard, with two coats of blackboard paint. As painting is usually messy, you will need to cover your child with a water-proof apron or overall, and protect the floor with newspaper or a plastic sheet. Exhibit your child's paintings and drawings around the house to make her feel proud and to encourage her to do more.

DRAWING EQUIPMENT

Useful equipment for drawing and painting includes: non-toxic paints and crayons; pencils and felt-tip pens; paint brushes of various sizes; cotton reels, potatoes, various shaped sponges for dip painting; non-spill paint pots; painting easel; wipe clean table; cover for clothes such as an apron or overall; supply of paper of various sizes, textures and colours for painting and drawing; chalks and blackboard; cardboard; colouring books.

SCRIBBLING AND DRAWING

By 15 months your child will be able to move her hands backwards and forwards to scribble. This is an important first step in her ability to control a pencil to write and draw. Chalks, crayons and pencils can be used for scribbling but chunky crayons are easier for young children to hold. Children's scribbling goes through various stages, and if you keep a copy of her scribble at various ages, you will see how it changes. Up to the age

of two, your child's scribble will be vigorous and all over the page, but from about two and a half, she may start to produce zigzags and lines. By the age of three, most children can draw straight lines and crosses, and your child may be able to copy a circle, some letters, or draw a face or a simple house. She should also be able to hold a crayon in a three-fingered grip, rather than in a fist, but pencil control varies and is often slower in boys than in girls. A fun way to teach your child to draw a face is by drawing one on her fingerpads and giving each one a name. Suggest your child lets them 'talk' to each other and make actions such as 'bowing' or 'waving'.

PAINTING

Make sure paint is non-toxic and provide it in a variety of colours. To minimise the risk of spills, stand pots of paint in a box, or use non-spill paint pots. Much of your child's painting is likely to be experimental at first – don't criticise her efforts but look at them with interest and ask her what they are meant to be. From the age of

BEING CREATIVE TOGETHER
Colouring in together with
your child will be rewarding
for both of you.

three, she may be able to copy simple shapes, some letters, and paint 'primitive' pictures.

Thick chubby brushes are best for younger children, but as she grows, finer ones will give her more satisfaction. Using a paintbrush and paper is not the only way for your child to paint. Items such as a nail brush, lolly sticks, sponge, feather or dish mop can also be used.

Finger painting Using her hands to make interesting designs on any smooth surfaced paper or other surface is a visual, physical and tactile experience for your child. For a young child show her the different effects she can make by using her fingers, heels of hands, palms, and so on. Make up actions such as pretending your child's hand is a bird and swooping it down to land on a 'lake' of blue paint. Or count your child's fingers as you put them one by one in the paint.

Foot painting Spread some large sheets of paper or plain wallpaper on a floor first covered with newspaper or a plastic sheet, and pour some finger paint on the paper. Tell your child the

colour or ask her what colour she wants. Let your child walk through it to make different effects. Hold a young toddler's hands in case she slips.

Blow painting Cover the immediate area with newspaper. Cut a drinking straw in half and put a blob of paint on a piece of plain white card or paper. Tell your child the colours of the paint and ask her which colour she wants, so that she learns the names. Let your child blow at the paint through the straw from different directions. When one colour is blown, add another colour of your child's choice.

Flick painting Drip some paint onto a piece of paper or cardboard and let your child flick it off.

Patterns Household objects such as combs, cotton reels, wedges of potato and cardboard tubes, and outdoor objects, such as stones and leaves, can be used to make patterns. Squeeze some blobs of paint onto a smooth surface and let your child run a comb through it to make a pattern. Or let her dip empty cotton reels or other objects in paint and press these onto paper.

Homemade finger paint

In a large saucepan dissolve 225 g (8 oz) cornstarch in a little cold water. Add 900 ml (1½ pints) boiling water. Return to heat and stir constantly until thick. Remove the mixture from the heat and stir in 40 g (1½ oz) pure white soap flakes or powder. Divide the mixture into small containers, allow to cool and add poster paint, water crayons or food colouring for colour.

Alternatively, liquid paint can be thickened with cornflour, flour, salt or crushed breakfast cereal, to create paints of different textures.

CREATIVE PLAY

Children love to make things and, if you have a variety of play materials readily available, you'll be able to give your toddler plenty of opportunity to develop her imagination, creativity and hand-eye coordination.

At first you will need to make things for your child, or provide her with a great deal of help, but eventually she will have the confidence and ability to be creative on her own. Use these occasions to talk to your toddler about what you are doing, and explain concepts such as shape, size, and colour. Once you have shown her what to do, let her get on with it herself. Admire her efforts and don't criticise.

MAKING COLLAGES

Collages are an ideal way for your toddler to experiment with and learn about different colours, shapes and textures. Using scissors and sticking things down will also give her practise in hand-eye coordination. Make sure the scissors your child uses are comfortable for her and have rounded ends. If she is left-handed get her left-handed scissors. By the time your toddler reaches the age of three, she should be able to cut out simple shapes with a blunt scissors. She will, however, need your help to cut out more intricate shapes or anything that requires the use of a sharper scissors such as cardboard. Let your toddler choose her own materials for the collage

and make up her own patterns. Younger children will find it much easier to first spread glue on the paper and then add the objects on top, rather than gluing these on individually.

Suggested materials A house and garden can provide a multitude of useable items such as dried pasta, egg cartons, cotton reels, cardboard tubes, paper bags, sticky paper, pebbles, leaves, milk bottle tops, doilies, old greetings cards, threads or wool, tin foil, dried beans and peas, tissue paper and yoghurt pots. You can use cardboard for a base or, for a different texture, try foil or velvet. Outdoors, encourage your child to collect different leaves, pebbles and flowers to use.

You can also buy sticky shapes, foils and coloured papers for your child to make into pictures, or glitter to decorate collages with.

Help your child to sort out all her bits and pieces into separate boxes or compartments so that she can easily find the things she needs.

Glue and paste Make sure that the glue your child uses is non-toxic and does not contain solvents. Never use strong instant adhesives that could bond to your child's fingers. Safe glues include glue sticks, wall paper paste or PVA glue, or you could make your own (see left). Plastic spreaders or wooden spatulas are easier to clean than brushes. 'Glitter glue' can be used in different colours to decorate cards and pictures.

Homemade glue

Bring to a rolling boil 180 ml (6 fl oz) water, 2 tablespoons of corn syrup, and 1 teaspoon of white vinegar. In a separate bowl mix together 125 g (4½ oz) cornstarch with 180 ml (6 fl oz) water. Slowly add this to the hot mixture, while constantly stirring to avoid lumps. Let it stand overnight before using.

BAGS AND BOXES OF FUN

Young children love putting things into and taking them out of bags and boxes, and these can also be used to make play things for them. Remember, however, to keep plastic bags well out of your child's reach and to forbid her to play with these.

★ Make a simple hand puppet by drawing eyes and a mouth on a paper bag. Cut a hole in the middle for your child's finger to act as a nose or cut each corner for two 'wiggly' ears.

★ Show her how to blow up and pop a paper bag.

★ Suspend a net bag filled with screwed up paper from a doorway or ceiling and let your child bash it with a wooden spoon.

★ Cover a shoe box with material or wallpaper to make a doll's cot or a storage box.

★ Cut holes in the top and sides of a large box to create the torso of a robot. Tie a piece of string to one end and let your child pull it along.

★ Cut holes for your child's legs in the bottom of an oblong box and make a car or bus. Let her paint 'wheels' on the side.

★ If your child is old enough give her some glue and let her construct models out of different sized boxes.

MODELLING DOUGH

Playing with modelling material gives your child lots of the opportunities to practise her manipulative and creative skills. Modelling dough or clay can be bought in toyshops or you can make your own. At first your child will just poke, slap, squeeze, or roll it, but soon she will make shapes that she perceives are animals, food and so on, even if these are indistinguishable to anyone else but herself. You may have to show her some simple shapes to start her off on her own ideas.

Working surfaces Your child can work on a piece of plastic laminate, smooth wood, or on a tray turned upside down, either sitting at a small table and chair or on the floor. You may wish to cover the floor with newspaper so that any dropped bits do not get trodden into the carpet.

Useful tools A small rolling pin, plastic biscuit cutters, small moulds such as bun trays or ice cube trays, child's blunt scissors, plastic fork for scratching patterns, plastic knives, plastic containers, and other small objects such as shells, dried pasta and beads which your child can push into the dough to make a pattern, will enable her to shape and decorate her dough.

Dough shapes Show your child how to make simple shapes such as balls and sausages which can be prodded and pounded into other shapes such as animals. She could also make pretend food such as cakes and biscuits. Or she could make dough faces – push in beans for eyes, macaroni for a mouth and to make hair, press some dough through a garlic press.

Homemade dough

Mix together in a large saucepan: 300 g (10½ oz) of plain flour, 325 g (11½ oz) salt, and 2 dessertspoons of cream of tartar. Add 600 ml (1 pint) of water, 2 tablespoons of oil, and a few drops of food colouring or powder paint gradually to the mixture and blend together with a wooden spoon. Cook the mixture gently over a low heat, stirring continually until it begins to thicken and becomes very stiff. Don't worry if the mixture gets lumpy as these disappear when the dough is kneaded. Scrape out the dough onto a clean surface and let it cool. Test before using to make sure that it is not too hot inside. The dough can be stored for several weeks in an airtight container or a plastic bag in the fridge.

Decorating the bedroom

Besides drawing and painting (see page 62), your child can also make various items to hang around her bedroom. Give her a variety of coloured cotton reels to thread onto various lengths of wool. Attach these to a coat hanger and hang it up as a mobile. Or, she could make some simple pictures by threading ribbon through cardboard with a very blunt needle.

Kids in the kitchen

Your child will love 'making things' in the kitchen with you – and it is a good opportunity to teach her about shapes, weighing, pouring, tastes, textures and colours. Making a jelly is simple and a good way to explain to your child how some substances dissolve in water. You can also explain how heat melts some substances while cooling allows them to set. Children who become involved in helping to prepare food are less likely to be fussy eaters. Let your child help get everything ready before starting and explain to her about the importance of washing her hands first. Afterwards, let her help you to 'wash up'.

Measuring, stirring and shaping When your child is about 18 months, you can measure out small quantities of ingredients such as flour, lentils, gravy powder, custard powder, sugar or rice in different bowls and let her mix them with water and a spoon.

THREADING
Give your child a few empty cotton reels and some coloured wool and you will be surprised how quiet it keeps him. Threading requires a lot of concentration for a toddler.

Let her feel the different textures with her hands, and make thicker ingredients such as flour, into little cakes. Let her help you make cakes by adding ingredients to the mixture and stirring this in the bowl. She could also have a go at rolling out dough for pastries or bread and cutting out biscuit shapes using plastic cutters.

Chopping and spreading By about the age of three your child will be able to use a blunt, round-ended knife for chopping soft foods such as bananas and soft cheeses and spreading bread with soft cheese, peanut butter or jam.

Decorating Let your child make her own butterfly sandwiches: cut sandwiches diagonally and reverse the halves. Spread these with cream cheese and let your child decorate them with raisins or pieces of soft fruit. Strips of pepper or vegetable sticks can be used as antennae. Pastry cutters can also be used for making fun-shaped sandwiches.

Chop up lots of different vegetables and grate some cheese and let your toddler add them to her own pizza base. You could give her pita bread so that she can make a child-sized pizza.

Provide your toddler with some hundreds-and-thousands, chocolate sprinkles, raisins and candied fruits and let her fashion her own biscuits or decorate buttered bread with these. Or she could add them to some ice-cream. She could try to make faces or different shapes.

IMAGINATIVE PLAY

Dressing up and taking on other roles enables your child to expand her creativity and allows her to practise her social skills by discovering how it feels to be someone else, and to consider their viewpoints. Through it she can express her fears or worries directly or indirectly, by playing out situations that may frighten her. Play such as this does not have to be expensive. Many props can be made out of household items.

Becoming a postman or woman
★ Save old letters for your child to 'deliver'.
★ Make a posting box out of a cardboard box.
★ Let her have an old shoulder bag as a sack.
★ Wrap up small empty packets for her to deliver.

Playing shop
★ Set up a shop counter with a cardboard box.
★ Give her net fruit bags for pretend shopping.
★ Provide small empty food boxes and small tins of food for the shop.

Doctors and nurses
★ Make a white apron out of old sheeting with tape sewn on and tie a white handkerchief or a teatowel round your child's head.
★ Cut down an old shirt into a doctor's white coat.
★ Make a stethoscope out of old headphones.

PLAY CORNERS
If you have space, screen or set aside a corner of the room which can become a 'tent' or 'house' for your child to play in. For example:
★ Make a 'bedroom' with a large laundry basket as a bed for your child to curl up in. Make a dressing table by tying a frill round the legs of a chair and tie a plastic mirror onto the back. Put old pots of make-up and a brush and comb on the chair seat, and perhaps a toy hairdryer.
★ To make a 'house' or 'tent' place two dining chairs back to back a short distance apart, place a broom across the seats and cover with a sheet; or place two armchairs back to back a short distance apart and drape an old blanket or sheet over them; or cover a table with an old sheet which reaches the ground on three sides at least.

DRESSING UP
Keep a dressing up box with old clothes and accessories with which your child can play. Make sure clothes are simple to put on, not too long to cause

*DRESSING UP FUN
A box full of your old clothes and costume jewellery will keep your child busy for hours.*

falls, and do not have any cords around the neck. Provide a long plastic or shatterproof mirror for your child to see herself dressed up. Include the following in the box: long skirts, tops, blouses, nighties, coats, old curtains, hats, scarves, gloves, belts, shoes, boots, handbags, shopping bags, rucksacks, sunglasses, straw hats, swimming things, umbrellas, raincoats, costume jewellery and old watches.

Household items can also be fun such as old plastic glasses, plastic cutlery, paper plates, pots and pans, chopsticks, rolling pins, plastic cutters.

Plait old tights together and sew them onto the side of a hairband to make imitation plaits.

Fill a small box with artificial flowers, old lace and feathers.

MUSIC AND MOVEMENT

Most children love singing, dancing and music. A young toddler will enjoy listening to different sounds and rhymes, and attempting actions such as clapping. From about the age of two he will attempt to join in songs and nursery rhymes. Making music does not have to be sophisticated – your child has probably already discovered satisfying noises he can make while playing – such as

HIS OWN DANCE
Your toddler may not yet be able to dance but he will enjoy doing all sorts of actions to music.

banging and rattling. At first he will need you to help him with movements and actions of songs, but as he gets older he will be able to attempt more difficult actions, such as jumping, himself. You may also want to introduce your child to a toddler music group and, when he is ready, let him start more formal music lessons.

Don't just restrict your child to children's songs and nursery rhymes. Let him have variety by listening to other music such as your own favourites, 'pop' songs or classical music.

MOVEMENT AND DANCE
Movement or dancing to music encourages the development of your child's motor skills, improves his balance, extends his range of movements, and helps to keep him physically fit.

Play music and walk with quick, slow, long and short steps, marching or walking on your toes and heels and let your child follow you. You can also dance with your child and, although he will be too young for formal dance lessons, he may enjoy going to movement classes.

MAKING MUSIC
If you have a musical instrument such as a piano or violin, play this to your child. There are also simple musical instruments you can buy for your young child to play, or you can make his own 'orchestra' using homemade instruments. Let your child experiment with making his own sounds.
Homemade instruments A variety of household equipment can be used by your child to make music: for example, banging on saucepans or tins with a wooden spoon, hitting a steel toast rack with a fork, clashing two saucepan lids together as cymbals, and rattling a bunch of keys.
To make shakers: Half fill empty plastic screw-topped jars with lentils, beans, rice or paper clips. If he is still putting things in his mouth, make sure these are well sealed. You or your child could also paint them in attractive colours.
To make drums: Cover a plastic dish or box with three layers of greaseproof paper or tin foil and secure this with an elastic band. Give your child a wooden spoon or small stick to hit it with.

MUSICIANS IN THE MAKING
Banging a saucepan 'drum' and shaking filled containers may not sound like music to your ears but provides fun and education for your toddler.

To make a harp: Stretch several rubber bands across a shoe box or tin.
Bells: Buy different types of bells and tie them onto thread or sticks for ringing.

LEARNING ABOUT SOUNDS

Making music can help your child's listening skills. Ask him to vary the sounds he makes, such as a hard beat on the 'drum', a soft shake and so on. Half-fill different sized plastic bottles with water and let your child beat them in turn to see what different sounds they make. When playing music to your child, you can also teach him to respond to changes in the music through movement or actions. For example, get him to stretch up high or jump for a high note; crouch down for a low note; or march or stamp to the different beats.

Imitating vocal sounds also plays an important part in teaching your child about music. Make lots of simple noises for him to copy, such as growling, grunting, and sounds such as 'oooooo', 'aaaaaaah' 'ssssssssh' etc.

Singing songs and nursery rhymes helps your child learn new words and develop his memory. There are many different types of children's songs and nursery rhymes available on cassette for your child to listen to. Encourage your child to join in the singing – if he is old enough, give him a large spoon to hold and pretend it's a microphone.

Songs with actions for young children

Children are more likely to enjoy songs that are accompanied by actions – there are many well-known nursery rhymes that can provide endless hours of entertainment as your child acts them out.

Encourage your toddler to sing and shout to his heart's content, if you can handle it.

All children love to sing "Ring a ring o' roses, A pocket full o' posies, A-tishoo! A-tishoo! We all fall down" as they hold hands, spin around and fall onto the ground. Younger toddlers should be given cushions to fall onto.

Some songs involve learning the body parts such as the *Hokey Cokey:* "put your right hand in, put your right foot out, you put your right hand in and shake it all about ..."

Songs such as *With my hands I clap clap clap, The wheels on the bus,* and *Here we go round the mulberry bush* have a range of actions to go with them.

WATER GAMES

Playing with water is fascinating for your toddler – it splashes, pours, drips, sprinkles, can be frozen, is hot, cold, and gives your toddler plenty of opportunities to learn. It is also cheap and convenient to provide. Baths, blowing bubbles, 'washing up' at the kitchen sink, paddling pools or a garden hose all offer opportunity for water play.

Dress your child in a plastic apron and roll his sleeves up, or take all his clothes off if it's warm. Keep some old towels nearby to mop up any splashes. Remember however, never leave your child to play alone with water – he can drown in only a few inches.

EXPERIMENTING WITH WATER

Many household items can be used as the basis for 'experiments'.

Sink or swim Fill a baby bath, the kitchen sink or a washing up bowl with water. Let your toddler put in stones, corks, plastic bottles, bath toys, a rubber ball and soap and see which of these will sink or float. Or play this game in the bath with a variety of toys – invent 'ships, pirates and sharks' to add to the fun.

Measure and pour Give him a number of different-sized measures and beakers and let him practise filling containers.

Treasure hunt Place some small bits of weeds or greenery from the garden in the bottom of a plastic container. Put some small stones or pebbles on top and some plastic sea animals if you have them. Hide a few small coins or small shiny objects amongst the stones. Fill the container with water. Colour the water blue or green with food colouring. Let your child hold a small plastic figure with moveable arms under the water (or a pair of tweezers) and see if he can find and pick up the treasures with it. Tell him to watch out for the sharks!

Making waves Fill a washing up bowl three quarters full with water. Then add washing up liquid and blue or green food colouring.

Give your child an egg whisk and let him make waves. Suggest he tries sailing a small boat, or anything that floats, such as bath toys, on the waves.

WASHING UP

Give him a bowl of warm soapy water and a washing up brush or cloth and ask him to help you do the dishes. Let him wash his own tea set, some plastic bowls or crockery, wooden spoons and teaspoons or other safe items. Give him his own rack to stack the items on when he has washed them.

BUBBLES

Blow bubbles to your child and let him try to catch them in his hands, or try breaking them by poking them with his finger or clapping them with his hands. Teach him to blow these himself, and let him see how far he can blow one. Dip the large end of a funnel in the solution and let your child blow large bubbles through the narrow end.

Making bubble solution

In a small plastic container or bowl pour 50 ml (2 fl oz) of clear washing up liquid or tear-free shampoo, 100 ml (3½ fl oz) of water and 2 teaspoons of glycerine (which makes the bubbles stronger). Make bubble blowers with various sized rings by twisting one end of a pipe cleaner, garden wire, or a piece of thin metal or plastic.

Bear in mind that some ready-made bubble solutions can leave stains on clothes.

HAVING A PARTY

It's fun to celebrate your toddler's birthday and by the age of two he will be able to appreciate it even though he may not fully understand what a party is. Serve savoury finger food first, such as crisps, small sausages, chunks of cheese and pineapple, tiny sandwiches cut into different shapes, mini pizzas, and raw vegetables cut into pieces. To follow, offer small portions of fruit, jelly, ice-cream, sweet biscuits and sweets. A cake shaped like a favourite nursery rhyme or television character will be appreciated.

FOR TWO-YEAR-OLDS

Talk to your toddler about the party a few days in advance, and about who will be coming. Keep the party fairly small and short at this age – an hour or an hour and a half will be long enough.

Protect your floor with a plastic cloth and fill cups only half full to avoid spills, or suggest that parents bring their child's own beaker with his name on. With young toddlers it is best to start serving the food very soon after they arrive. Play some nursery rhyme tapes for background music.

Activities Most two-year-olds are too young to play party games, but will enjoy 'dancing' to nursery rhymes, playing 'ring-a-ring o' roses' or doing other simple action songs. They will also enjoy playing simple musical instruments such as shakers (see page 68).

FOR THREE-YEAR-OLDS

A party lasting one and a half to two hours will be long enough for three-year-olds. It's a good idea to alternate energetic games with quieter ones. Try to play at least one game where every child wins a prize.

Pass the parcel Wrap a small prize in several layers of newspaper and sticky tape. Let the children sit on the floor in a circle and pass the parcel round to music. When the music stops the child who has the parcel unwraps as many layers as possible until the music starts again.

Treasure hunt For each child wrap a simple prize such as a bar of chocolate in bright paper and tie it to a long length of coloured wool. Hide the parcels and trail the wool lengths around the room. Give each child a length of wool and send them off to find their treasure.

Musical statues The children walk or move to music, and when it stops they stand still. Rather than eliminating children from the rounds, give a small prize to the first one to stand still or the funniest statue until everyone has a prize.

PARTY TIPS

★ Arrange for a few adults to help you.
★ Stock up on wet wipes and paper towels, for mopping up spills and sticky children.
★ Keep a supply of spare pants in case of accidents. Remind the children to go to the toilet – with all the excitement they might forget.
★ Don't mix the age range of the children you are inviting as this is bound to lead to fights and tears.
★ Don't invite more than you can accommodate.

JOINING IN
Your three-year-old will probably be excited by the idea of a party and is now old enough to decide who to ask, and to help with the invitations and some simple food preparations.

OUTDOOR PLAY AND EXCURSIONS

Exercising in the fresh air helps to keep your toddler physically fit and healthy. Outdoor physical activities such as running, jumping, climbing, swinging and throwing, help children to develop balance and coordination and a knowledge of distance, height and space. It also provides a necessary outlet for their boundless energy. If possible, let your child work off some of his energy outdoors everyday.

Not all outside play or activities, however, have to be physical. There are also opportunities outdoors for your child to learn about nature and to develop his creativity and imagination.

Excursions will also broaden your child's mind – but whether they consist of short trips to the supermarket on public transport or overseas holidays, being well prepared ahead of time can make them more of a success.

PHYSICAL ACTIVITIES
Children should have opportunities to play outdoors on equipment which develops physical coordination. A small climbing frame or slide offers practise for your child to gain control over his movements, such as deciding where to put his arms and feet, and to use his body in a number of ways. If you buy a frame, try to get one with extra attachments that can be added as your child grows. A set of sturdy boxes, short planks and

THE YOUNG GARDENER
Expand outdoor activities – provide opportunities for your toddler to develop an appreciation of nature.

FUN AND EXERCISE
A tricycle will give your toddler the chance to expend energy and learn coordination.

short ladders can also be put together to be climbed over, into, or made into an obstacle course. A plank put over a couple of house bricks can also be used for practising balancing. A low swing will also offer your child opportunities to practise, or show off, his skills. If you don't have the space to provide large outdoor equipment, visit the local park regularly.

Toys you can easily offer your child include balls for throwing and kicking and tricycles. Always bear safety in mind when buying equipment or when your child is playing in public spaces (see page 55).

NATURE PLAY
If you have a garden, your child will probably love to help you in it, and enjoy having his own set of miniature tools and a wheelbarrow. If possible, let him have a spare piece of ground in which to dig himself, or to grow seeds. But you will need to explain that seeds take a long time to grow into flowers. He can also help you to rake up leaves. Remember, however, to be careful about garden safety (see page 55).

When going for walks, look out for things to collect for later use to make collages or leaf prints,

SAND PLAY
Playing with sand provides
both creative stimulation
and practice in hand-eye
coordination.

or as a nature display. Horse chestnuts, stones, pebbles, shells, seaweed, driftwood, acorns, feathers, leaves, pine cones, or grasses are all collectable. Your own garden is also stocked with wildlife such as birds and insects. Help your child to identify these and talk about their sizes and colours. Explain that insects are eaten by birds, but that they are not suitable for children to eat!

Water, sand and mud are all materials that your child will enjoy playing with in the garden. A sand pit can be bought ready-made, or you can make one out of an old container. Silver sand is best as builder's sand will stain clothes. The same kinds of containers used for water play can be used in dry sand. Take care that a young child does not rub sand in his eyes, and make it a rule that sand is never thrown at anyone. Always cover the sand pit over when not in use to protect it from rain and cats.

Although messy, most children love playing with mud. Dress your child in old clothes and wellington boots, and make a mud pit for him similar to a sand pit.

WET WEATHER ACTIVITIES

Rain or snow should not preclude outdoor activities. Dress your child in suitable clothes and take him outside for some play or a short walk if possible, even on rainy or snowy days. Go on a puddle hunt in the rain and let him splash through these in wellington boots. Point out the differently shaped clouds and ask him what animals he thinks they look like. Look for his reflection in puddles. If you see a rainbow ask him if he can name any colours. Encourage him to stick his tongue out to taste the rain or snow, or icicles. If it has snowed, let him throw

snowballs at a wall or have a mock snowball fight. Build a snowman together and let your child name him, and dress him with a hat and scarf. Go around the garden looking for bird tracks or let him make his own footprints.

EXCURSIONS AND OUTINGS

Even everyday outings such as going to the park, are learning experiences for your child. There is also the pleasure of doing fun things such as feeding the ducks, playing on equipment or running around. Even before you get to your destination, you will have opportunities to discuss with your child the things you are seeing, such as dogs, buses, or goods in shop windows.

For impulse outings, or to save time generally, keep a small bag packed ready with items such as a couple of disposable nappies, a spare pair of pants, baby wipes, tissues, some plastic bags for rubbish, small cartons of juice and a beaker.

If your toddler is very active, don't go anywhere where he will be confined to his buggy for too long. If your child is old enough, let him carry a lightweight rucksack with a favourite toy and book, and his own drink and snack.

LOCAL VISITS

When taking everyday walks, try to vary familiar routes so that your child sees new things. Add to your child's experiences by including interesting places to visit, taking into account your child's age and personality. For example, a visit to the local pet shop might lead to a day at the zoo or a farm. Talk to your child about the animals, what they are, the sounds they make and so on. Keep the visits short to avoid boredom. When you get home, look through an animal book and see if

DOS AND DON'TS FOR OUTINGS

✔ Do keep safety in mind: use reins or a pushchair.

✔ Do pre-plan your trip and try to avoid very long journeys.

✔ Do allow lots of time to get to where you want to go if walking – toddlers love to dawdle and stop to look.

✔ Do take a variety of snacks and drinks with you.

✘ Don't be embarrassed to ask other people for help with pushchairs.

✘ Don't travel in peak hours if possible.

Going shopping with your toddler

Shopping for food or other essentials with a lively or bored young child in tow, is an experience many parents would prefer to miss, but can't avoid. You may need to try several strategies to prevent shopping being a hassle.

- Decide on the rules that suit you, such as never buying sweets in supermarkets, and stick to them.
- Try to go to the supermarket when it's quiet.
- Try to make it a learning experience by involving your child in choosing food that you are going to buy – for instance, does he want red or green apples, or what flavour yoghurt. If he picks up unsuitable food, decide whether you are going to explain why you don't want it, or whether it's easier to put it back when he's not looking. If he is old enough, let him for look for items on the shopping list. You could draw pictures of some of these and ask your child to remind you what they are.

- Try to shop when you or your child is not tired or hungry – or carry a suitable snack such as a bun or banana, which he can eat if necessary.
- Visit stores with the best toilet and changing facilities.
- Take your child to a small specialist shop such as a butcher's sometimes so that he can see close up how food is cut up or weighed.
- If you have a lot of shopping to do, try and break up the time with a visit to a café or see if a crêche is available.

your child can spot the animals he saw. If you live near an airport or railway station, your child will enjoy going to look at the planes taking off or landing, to the station to see the trains or, if you live near the sea or a river, going on a boat trip.

TRAVELLING

Going for an outing on a bus or train is an adventure for your child but can involve extra effort for you. On escalators, make sure your child stands on the complete step and has no trailing garments that could get caught. If you are taking the buggy, try to avoid carrying too many other things. A large shoulder bag or a rucksack which holds all you need is best. Take your time getting on and off the bus, and beware of automatic doors. Ask other passengers to help if necessary. Have plenty of small change for fares and try to have the right fare money ready before you board. Keep your child well back from the platform at underground and train stations and watch him closely.

You can get a bicycle with a seat on the back, and take your toddler for rides. Make sure that his feet are well away from the wheels and that he wears a protective helmet.

If travelling by plane, find out what facilities the airline has before you book.

Earache may affect your child on takeoff or landing – give him a drink or something to chew during take off or landing, or his dummy to suck if he normally uses one.

Food for your child when travelling Young children need to eat fairly frequently and depending on how far you are going, try to have a variety of food or snacks and drink available. Good choices include small sandwiches, savoury or plain sweet biscuits (ginger ones may help to prevent travel sickness), chunks of hard cheese and pineapple in a container, fresh fruit such as bananas, seedless satsumas, or cut-up apples, raisins or seedless grapes, and raw vegetable sticks such as carrots, celery and peppers in a plastic container. Avoid food that could cause tummy upsets if kept warm, such as cream, meat or fish. A vacuum flask of iced water is a good idea. Disposable bibs are very convenient.

Changing your child If your child is not yet potty trained, an adequate supply of disposable nappies is essential for travelling, along with a supply of baby wipes, and nappy sacks or plastic bags with ties to put the nappy in. If your child is still being potty trained, a travel potty with a lid, or an inflatable potty with disposable liners can be used.

Toys and games Take your child's favourite toys (but take care they do not get lost), sing-along cassette tapes and stories, and suitable travel games to help prevent boredom on the journey. Play games such as how many red buses, dogs, or petrol stations you can spot.

Travel sickness Many young children experience travel sickness when travelling in cars, trains, boats or planes. Symptoms include nausea, vomiting, dizziness, sweating and headache. Your child may become pale and go very quiet before being sick. Travel sickness is caused by the repeated movement of the vehicle affecting the body's balancing system which is situated in the inner ear. Other causes include anxiety and excitement, a stuffy atmosphere, smells such as petrol or smoke, a too full or an empty stomach, and focusing on near objects such as books. Here are some tips to help prevent travel sickness or to make the aftermath more pleasant.

★ Give your child a light meal before the journey, but avoid fizzy drinks, greasy foods and chocolate.

★ Drugs are available to prevent travel sickness but check with your pharmacist which products and what doses are appropriate for your child's age, and for how long the relief will last. Medications which can cause drowsiness may be useful for a long journey during the night. If your child is under two and suffers from travel sickness, you may be able to obtain a prescription from the doctor.

Alternatively, you could give your child a homeopathic travel sickness remedy.

*OUT AND ABOUT
Let your toddler take her own little bag with some favourite items to make her feel truly grown-up.*

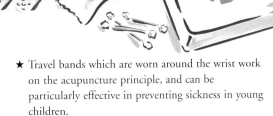

★ Travel bands which are worn around the wrist work on the acupuncture principle, and can be particularly effective in preventing sickness in young children.

★ Keep your child busy, but avoid any games that involve reading.

★ Keep the car well ventilated, and avoid smoking.

★ Stop for short periods whenever you can, to let your child have some fresh air and stretch his legs.

★ Keep a plastic bucket and lid, moist wipes, tissues and a towel handy.

★ If your child is sick, a damp cloth sprinkled with bicarbonate of soda will take away the worst of the smell.

★ Keep a change of clothes in the car.

YOUR TODDLER'S EMOTIONAL NEEDS

As your child matures from a baby to a more independent person, the world can become more of a bewildering and confusing place. As he develops more awareness of himself and others he will experience and demonstrate a wide range of emotions. You will need to respond effectively to these changes providing comfort or discipline as necessary.

ENCOURAGING INDEPENDENCE

To encourage your child to become more independent, it is important to build up his self-confidence from an early age. Give him lots of love and attention and use positive reinforcement whenever he achieves something. Don't ever make him feel like a failure for his inability to do something as this is likely to inhibit him from making new attempts at that task.

PROMOTING INDEPENDENCE
Encouraging your child to become involved in a range of activities will help him to become more independent. The more stimulation and opportunity to develop new skills that he has, the more likely he is to feel confident at doing things on his own. Playing a variety of games, alone as well as with other children, visiting public places and other people's homes all help to increase the range of your toddler's knowledge and experience.

Socialisation is also important for becoming independent (see page 30). In addition, there are many daily routines such as getting dressed which provide perfect opportunities to encourage your child's independence, while

DON'T BE INTRUSIVE
Take an interest in your child's play activities and help him if necessary, but avoid taking over or interfering.

enhancing his physical and intellectual development at the same time.

★ Allow him to make decisions sometimes such as choosing his own clothes to wear.
★ Allow him to do things for himself even if he makes mistakes at first.
★ Avoid being dominant and always taking the lead when you play with him. Play games such as 'Follow the leader' and let him be leader.
★ Include your child in adult conversations and avoid 'talking over his head'.
★ Make deliberate silly mistakes such as cutting up food with a spoon, or emptying food from an unopened tin, and let your child correct you.
★ Encourage him to discuss his feelings and ideas.
★ Apologise to him when you've been unfair.
★ If your child is shy, encourage him to join small groups, but don't force him to join in.

LEAVING YOUR CHILD
At some stage, you and your child will need to separate from each other. This may be a short break or a much longer period if you plan to return to work and you have to leave your child with a childminder or at a day care centre. Separations are likely to be very difficult for you both, particularly if you are unprepared. And of course, the more upset one of you feels, the more likely the other is to

GROWING UP
Let your child help you with the housework even if his help is more of a hindrance. Imitating adults is an important part of gaining independence.

become upset too. So it is better all round to plan the separation carefully.

You may have already left your child with a relative or trusted babysitter for a few hours when he was younger but once he is older, he may develop more fears and insecurities that must be addressed. It is essential that you tell him often that you will see him soon – the most common fear children have when left with a childminder is that mummy or daddy is not coming back. Once your toddler firmly believes that you will return, he can turn his attention to his new surroundings.

Preparing for separation It is a good idea to take your child to a playgroup regularly so that he gets used to mixing with other children and to being around other adults. Once he has learnt to socialise he will be much less likely to notice you are not around.

Start to leave him for an hour or two with a trusted friend or relative, preferably someone with whom he is already comfortable. As he gets used to your absence, increase the amount of time you spend away from him.

Choosing a childminder or day care centre
Don't leave it to the last minute to select your child's carer as this is one of the most important decisions you can make and requires some thought and research.

★ Prepare a list of questions that you want to ask then go and see several childminders or centres. If you are not sure about something, phone and ask again.

★ Always choose a registered childminder or centre. Seek recommendations.

★ Check that other children there seem happy and involved in activities. Are they being properly supervised?

★ Make sure that meals are nutritious.

★ Take your child to visit your chosen centre and let him get used to it while you are present.

The first day Explain very positively to your toddler the day before what will happen at the centre – don't let on if you are anxious. If possible, arrive early so that your toddler can settle in before you have to leave for work. Expect a lot of tears when you leave but don't allow yourself to feel guilty – most toddlers adjust to separation quickly. Tell the childminder or day care centre your child's likes and dislikes, including favourite foods and words used for going to the toilet.

On your return home, make sure you give your child plenty of attention. Ask him what he has done that day and be aware of his feelings. If he seems unhappy you will have to weigh up whether it is temporary or whether there are serious concerns about his care.

PREPARING YOUR TODDLER
Getting your child used to other adults will go a long way towards preparing him to be left alone with one.

FRUSTRATIONS OF GROWING UP

Most parents would like their child to be good, polite, sociable and well behaved. It can therefore come as quite a shock if your happy, compliant baby, turns almost overnight into a whinging, disobedient, aggressive, overactive, or temper prone toddler, whose favourite word is 'no' and with whom life has become a power struggle. Of equal concern to parents is a child who, compared to other children her age, seems full of fears, is shy or clingy, who gets bullied, or whose 'comfort' habits make her parents feel uncomfortable or embarrassed.

Just as no parent is perfect, all children behave badly or are difficult from time to time. And what may constitute bad behaviour in one family, may be accepted as normal in another. Remember there is no one correct way to bring up a child.

It is also normal for a young child to test you to your limits, to go through a negative stage, to ignore what you said, and to want to be the centre of attention. But all children need limits set to their behaviour and to learn what is or is not acceptable. An uncooperative or physically aggressive child who bullies other children, or one who is totally uncontrolled, becomes unpopular and socially isolated. She also becomes unhappy

within herself and feels unwanted and her behaviour may worsen.

The personality or temperament of your child is also an important factor in her behaviour and how you deal with it. For example, some children seem to be born with an easy-going and friendly disposition, or a placid personality. Others are more determined to question and challenge everything, or get excited easily and will never sit still. Or, if a child is 'extra special', perhaps because she was premature or seriously ill as a baby, parents may find it more difficult to lay down rules about their child's behaviour. If you are having problems coping with your child's behaviour, or feel her behaviour is getting worse, you may need to think carefully about whether the problem is yours, rather than hers. Factors such as feeling stressed or tired, or bringing up your child alone can all affect how you react to her behaviour. Also, most parents at some point have negative feelings about their child – you just have to recognise when you are feeling this way and try to take some time out from parenting.

Leave your child with a friend or relative she knows well and do something just for you. If it is impossible for you to get away for a whole day, try to at least get a childminder for a couple of hours so that you can calm yourself down. If you feel that you are persistently feeling or behaving negatively towards your child, you should seek advice from your doctor or health visitor.

SEE THINGS HER WAY

If you look at life from a toddler's point of view, you can see how it can be very irritating and frustrating. She has learnt to walk and climb, and the world has become full of interesting and exciting opportunities, with so much for her to see and explore. But just when she heads for an open cupboard filled with bottles and boxes to pull out, someone locks the door. She may see a handbag on the floor or table which looks similar to the one she has in her toy box – but is told 'that's naughty' if she empties it out. She is now able to 'help' mum around the house with the dusting, but mum may get cross when she tries to be helpful and unpacks and spills the shopping.

HUG ME
Very often your child's frustrating behaviour is just her own way of saying 'pay attention to me'.

WHY NOT?
A handbag provides a delightful opportunity to explore the unknown and touch and probably chew interesting objects. From a toddler's point of view there is no reason why a handbag should be left alone – after all isn't it just another toy mum left on the table?

Parenting tips

- Try to deal with your own stress before you start to deal with your child.
- Love is your child's most important need. Never tell your child that you don't love her.
- Give your child your full attention when she's telling you something.
- Always be consistent with your child.
- Most children from 18 months to three years can be frustrating – yours is not the only one!
- Praise good behaviour.
- To help deal with your child's difficult behaviour, keep a note of when it occurs, and see if you can pinpoint the cause.
- Give your child choices when you can.
- If you have to say no, try to explain why.
- Try not to pick fights about little things.
- If you get it wrong, say so and apologise.
- Try to stay in control -- remember you're supposed to be the mature one, not your child.

She is given some household items to play with, but the other interesting looking objects that she wants, are put firmly out of her reach.

She is congratulated when she climbs onto a chair to sit at the table. But when she climbs to look through an open window, to see what's going on outside, she is hauled down. She is given some crayons and paper to draw on, and her efforts are admired. But when she expands her artistic merits to draw across the wallpaper, this is not appreciated by her parents. When she wants to go to the park to play, she is made instead to go to a boring supermarket. There she is not allowed to run around or touch things, and has to wait for what seems hours in an endless queue with nothing to do.

Her parents may also be inconsistent or disagree on house rules. Dad does not mind if she comes back down after being put to bed, but mum always objects – who does she take notice of? Mum lets her choose what t-shirt to put on, but dad expects her to wear whatever he brings out first. Sometimes, if mum is in a good mood, she will let her have the sweets in the supermarket, but other times she doesn't. Or dad always buys her some and mum gets cross about it.

Then there's the language problem! She knows what she wants, or she wants to tell you how she feels, but it's hard for her to explain if she's not quite talking in sentences (see page 26). And one word she is probably hearing constantly now is 'no'. 'No, you can't play with the video. No, don't

NO, NO, NO
Defensive body language comes as naturally to a child as to an adult – crossed arms and a pouting face are a sure indication your toddler is about to say 'no'.

pull the cat's tail, it's naughty. No, come down from that table, you'll fall. No, don't touch the kettle, it's hot. No, you can't have Jamie's toy, it's not yours.' Small wonder then that 'no' also becomes a toddler's favourite word.

Because a child is the centre of her own world, it is also understandable that as she learns that life has its limitations, and that she can't have or do everything she wants, frustration sometimes breaks out into a temper tantrum.

A temper tantrum is when your child is in an uncontrolled rage. Most children between the ages of 18 months and three years have them occasionally but some have them more frequently than others. They are more common in strong willed or determined children than those who are placid and easy-going. In some children a tantrum may be a short outburst of rage which soon blows over. In others it may last for some time, with the child lying on the ground screaming and kicking, throwing things or holding his breath. Having an occasional temper tantrum may actually be good for your child's emotional development. It can release his pent up frustration, and teach him that feeling anger is normal, but that its expression needs to be controlled. It also means that your child has energy and assertiveness that will stand him in good stead later on. But too many tantrums are exhausting for parents and child and become antisocial behaviour. So if your child has tantrums frequently try to work out the reason why and as far as possible, avoid these trigger situations.

HOLDING BREATH

It is not unusual for toddlers to hold their breath when in a temper. The child becomes redder and redder and then turns blue or may turn white. The breathing usually starts again at this stage, but sometimes the child goes stiff or floppy or may even pass out. Seeing your child holding his breath is very frightening, but fortunately will not harm him. If he goes unconscious after breath-holding, check with your doctor to exclude any medical cause. Otherwise, difficult though it is,

WATCH ME SCREAM Often a small event can trigger your toddler into a tantrum when you least expect it. Watch for the warning signs on his face.

ignore your child when he holds his breath – don't slap him or pour cold water on him. If he does become briefly unconscious, watch him carefully, but move away as soon as he starts to come round.

HEAD BANGING

Between the ages of one and two, if a child does not have his own way or gets into a temper tantrum, he may bang his head against the wall or floor. Although parents worry that the child will hurt himself, injury is rare. If your child is otherwise normal, head banging is nothing to worry about and best ignored. Some children may also head bang before going to sleep, or if they are tired or bored (see page 87).

CAUSES OF TEMPER TANTRUMS

Attention seeking behaviour Toddlers love to be the centre of attention, and throwing a tantrum may be one way of achieving this.

Frustration This may result if your child is not allowed to do something he wants to do, he is unable to do something due to limited capabilities, or if he is made to do something he does not want to do. Pick your battles, and don't fight over small things that do not really matter, such as objecting to him wearing odd socks or not letting him pick what t-shirt to wear.

Imitation He may see and copy another child or adult having a tantrum.

THROWING THINGS Once a tantrum starts anything at hand might go flying. Remove breakables from his reach.

Blackmail He may use a tantrum as a device to get his own way.

Tiredness Tantrums are more common if a child is tired or overexcited.

Hunger Children need to eat regularly, and if mealtimes are too far apart your child may get hungry. Make sure he gets some nourishing snacks in-between meals (see page 9).

Inconsistency Allowing him to do some things, but not others, without any clear guidelines, or one parent saying 'yes', and the other 'no' is confusing and frustrating for your toddler. Don't expect too much from your toddler, and build in a rest time during the day. If you pack too many activities into a day, or expect him to accompany you shopping if he's been busy at playschool or at the child care centre, then an explosion is more likely.

DEALING WITH TANTRUMS

As far as possible, try to identify trigger situations and avoid them. But if your child does throw a tantrum, try to keep calm and remember that in time he will get over this phase.

As he gets older you will be able to talk more about angry feelings, and ways of coping with these. Meanwhile, don't lose your own temper or give in, and don't try to deal with the tantrum using bribes, smacking or threats.

★ **Distract** Try pointing out of the window at something or suggest going to the park.

★ **Ignore** If your child does not have an audience, he cannot perform. Put him in a different room until the tantrum is over or, if he is safe, you leave the room.

★ **Removal** If out in public, decide whether to stay put until the tantrum blows over and ignore any disapproving comments or looks, or whether to physically remove him from the scene with the least possible fuss. If your child is kicking and screaming, move any potentially dangerous objects out of his reach, so that he cannot hurt himself.

★ **'Angry toys'** Provide your child with alternative outlets for anger and frustration – toys such as drums or other musical instruments may help him work out his feelings and channel them in constructive ways, as will physical activities such as riding a tricycle. Encourage him to express himself through drawing.

★ **Joining in** If your child is shouting, join in for a while, then gradually lower your voice – your child will probably copy you until you are both whispering. This will help show your child that anger is more acceptable expressed in words, than in physical violence.

★ **Make up** Once the tantrum is over, let your child know that it is natural to feel angry and that you feel angry too sometimes. Make sure he knows that you still love him and that it is his behaviour you don't like. Remember to congratulate him once he has regained control.

TANTRUM TIME
Only hold your child if you are strong enough to do so and if you feel this is the right thing to do. A struggling child can be hard to contain.

AGGRESSIVENESS

Anger and aggression are common in toddlers from around the age of two and are very closely linked. Aggressiveness, however, is usually seen as a more extreme form of anger and is directed against someone else. A toddler may hit, bite, scratch or kick another child, an adult, or an animal. A young child displaying aggression can cause parents a great deal of anxiety and concern, and such behaviour is unpopular with other parents and children. But if your toddler is sometimes aggressive, this does not mean that he is going to grow up aggressive or antisocial.

Frustrations that are minor to an adult, can be major to a toddler and result in a physical reaction. So most young children will occasionally hit or bite someone or to give another toddler a shove. A young toddler may also poke someone's eyes, bite, or pull hair out of natural curiosity and because he does not know that it hurts. It is also normal for a two-year-old not to want to share, to be possessive about his toys and fight with other children over these. Boys are thought to be more aggressive than girls though whether this is instinctive or learned behaviour is a subject for debate.

Nevertheless, if your toddler starts showing aggressive behaviour and bullies other children, he needs to understand that this behaviour is unacceptable and you need to help him to learn other ways of dealing with his rage and expressing himself.

CAUSES OF AGGRESSIVE BEHAVIOUR

Your toddler may become angry because he is:

★ Being prevented from doing something he wants to do, or having difficulty in being understood.
★ Is too young to understand that certain physical actions can hurt.
★ Feeling emotionally stressed, insecure or unloved.
★ Feeling jealous, such as after the arrival of a new baby (see page 90).
★ Imitating an adult or older child who is aggressive towards him.
★ Reacting to certain foods and additives (see page 89).
★ Disturbed by a physical problem such as a hearing impairment (see page 38).
★ Tired and hungry.
★ Boisterous – such children may express their energy and enthusiasm in a more aggressive way than shy or placid children.
★ Not being able to let off steam through physical outdoor activities (see page 72).
★ Watching violent or aggressive television characters getting away with their behaviour.
★ Experiencing continual criticism or punishment.

OUCH!
Many toddlers go through a phase of displaying aggressive behaviour such as hitting and biting. When it is ongoing, your toddler must be told it is unacceptable.

CURBING AGGRESSIVE BEHAVIOUR

At the first sign of negative behaviour you need to react. If your toddler bites, hits or kicks you or another child, make it clear that this hurts and you won't allow him to do it again. If it happens to a child when you are in a group or your child is playing with another, tell your child that you will leave or will ask his playmate to leave if he does it again. Then make a great fuss of the victim and ignore your child. If your warning is ignored and the aggression is repeated, carry out your threat. If the behaviour is directed at you and you are at home, remove your child from the scene and place him in another room for a short period (see page 95).

Some parents, when confronted with aggressive behaviour, may feel that smacking is the only solution, but this can teach children that violence is acceptable. However, a quick and painless smack with the hand to show your child that he is wrong is considered acceptable by some people.

If you are seriously concerned about your child's aggression, talk to your doctor or health visitor.

PREVENTING AGGRESSION

Keep an eye on your child when he's playing with other children. As with temper tantrums, a child who is about to display aggressive behaviour can sometimes be distracted. For example, if a fight is about to break out with another young toddler over a toy, take it away from both, and distract them with another activity. A sharp 'no' to a child who is about to bite or kick, may halt him in his tracks, or try giving instructions in a loud voice such as; 'Jamie hug' or 'Jamie kiss Jane.'

However, don't always rush to break up a dispute between three-year-olds unless it looks like one will get hurt – it is best if they can resolve this themselves.

If your child is not yet into sharing, put away his favourite toys when another child comes to play to avoid a dispute.

If your child is getting overexcited when playing, calm him down with a break for a drink or snack. On the other hand, if he hasn't had sufficient activity to let off steam, let him dance or run around some of the day.

In a quiet moment talk to your child to try to find out if anything is worrying him. He may be jealous of a new baby, or be feeling upset about a change in his life. As he grows older, show your

KISS AND MAKE UP
Toddlers may quickly turn from playing happily to aggressive fighting when a favoured toy is at stake. If the toddlers are usually good friends then very often you can persuade them to kiss and make up. They may be a little chilly at first but this will soon turn into a game itself.

child how to be assertive and expressive without being aggressive.

When your child's being aggressive, make it clear that it's his behaviour that you don't like and not him. He is probably feeling very unhappy about his behaviour, and needs your reassurance that he is still loveable.

BULLYING

Even children as young as three can be bullies, and may single out a particular child to torment. It is important to take action and not think the bad behaviour will just go away. If you think your child is being a bully, you need to find out the reason – jealousy, low self esteem, frustration, or someone else may be bullying your child (see pages 85).

FEARS AND INSECURITY

A child who is anxious, afraid, unsure, lacks confidence, or feels she is not adequately protected will be insecure. Most young children suffer a certain amount of insecurity at some stage and some children are more naturally timid and anxious than others. It is normal for young children to cling to an adult, usually their mother, when anxious, tired or upset. It is also normal if toddlers become distressed when their mothers leave them somewhere strange, such as a new playgroup or childminder.

Young children are also continuously fearful about the dark, insects, dogs, thunder storms, water, noise from machines such as vacuum cleaners, ghosts, getting lost or being abandoned and so on. Insecurity, however, may be caused by the following:

★ A new baby in the family.
★ Too much or too little discipline.
★ Inconsistent discipline from her parents.
★ Fear of starting playgroup or nursery.
★ Illness or depression in either parent.
★ Parental conflict.
★ Overemphasis on things such as keeping clean and tidy, good behaviour or being toilet trained.
★ Fears and worries passed on by an adult.
★ Low self esteem.
★ Too many changes in her life.

A TEARY CHILD
Your child may go through a phase of frequent bouts of crying without obvious reason. He may be feeling insecure or experiencing various fears which he cannot communicate. It is important to give him reassurance.

As your child matures she will become less clingy and outgrow many of her fears. But it is important to recognise where insecurities are caused by your behaviour, and to take the appropriate actions to remedy it.

HELP YOUR CHILD TO FEEL SECURE
Never laugh at your child's fears or tell her she is silly. Remember, many adults are also afraid of thunder, the dark and spiders. Acknowledge and sympathise with her fears and think of ways to help her overcome them. For instance, if she is afraid of dogs reassure her that you will protect her. Tell her that she is right not to be friendly with strange dogs, but help her to gradually get to know some friendly ones. If she is afraid of the dark, provide her with a night light for as long as she wants it, and if necessary, do a ritual check for 'monsters' under the bed or in the wardrobe.

Expose her to a wide range of experiences and activities outside her home and meet and mix with other adults and children.

Never slip away and leave your child without telling her that you are going. If you do leave her with someone else or at a playgroup, tell her

SCARY MACHINES
A child may fear being sucked into a vacuum cleaner. You can help her to overcome this fear by demonstrating that even when the nozzle is pressed against her it can't suck her in.

when you are going, even if this does mean some tears. Also tell her when you will be back. Let her take her favourite comforter with her to a new situation, even if it makes you feel embarrassed (see page 86).

Don't push your child away if she clings to you. This will make her even more anxious and cling all the more. Treat it sympathetically as a phase which will pass and allow your child to become more independent in her own time.

Never threaten to leave your child, in anger or in jest. Fear of abandonment is one of the greatest anxieties your child can experience and can result in long-term insecurity. Your child needs to know that you are always there for her, no matter how badly she has behaved.

Try not to transmit your own fears, insecurities and anxieties to your child as she is likely to copy these.

Make sure you praise and reassure your toddler often and focus on her strong points.

Don't expect too much too soon. Remember that confidence builds up gradually.

Finally, do not talk to friends or relatives about her fears or shyness in front of her as this will make her more self-conscious.

HELPING A SHY CHILD MAKE FRIENDS

If your child is quiet or shy, you may worry about whether she will make friends or join in activities with other children when she goes to nursery or playgroup. Once she has got used to group activities she will probably become more outgoing and confident, but trying to 'jolly' her into something she is not yet ready to handle may make the situation worse. Point out that the other children seem to be having fun and gently encourage her to join in but, until she is ready to do so, let her watch from the sidelines for as long as she needs to. If she finds joining in with a group difficult, you could also ask one or two of the children home to play.

Is your child being bullied?

Fears and insecurity may indicate that your child is being bullied or teased, although this is hard to confirm if she is too young to tell you. If you suspect she has a problem, you could ask her to tell you all the nice things that happened to her that day and then all the 'nasty things'. Or you could ask her to draw you some pictures of what happens at playgroup.

Signs of bullying
- Reluctance to attend playgroup, nursery or to play at certain friends' houses.
- Becoming more clingy.
- Getting upset easily or becoming tearful.
- Complaining of stomach pains or loss of appetite.
- Bed wetting after becoming dry.
- Not sleeping well or having nightmares.
- Frequent bruises or scratches.
- Any very out-of-character behaviour.

Helping your child overcome bullying
- Build up her self-confidence.
- Teach your child to be assertive without being aggressive.
- Teach her ways to deal with the immediate situation such as by walking away from a bully, shouting 'no', or telling an adult.

- Reassure her that it's not her fault.
- Speak to the playgroup or nursery leader and, if the behaviour persists, to the bullying child's parents.
- If you are present, intervene at once and tell the other child that his behaviour is not acceptable.
- Give your child lots of comfort and cuddles if she has been hurt.
- Encourage her to tell you when something is bothering her.

A CLINGY CHILD
A child who has become far more clingy than usual may be being bullied or experiencing other sources of insecurity.

COMFORTERS AND COMFORT HABITS

A comforter is any item that a child may use to make her feel happier or more secure, for example, a piece of cot blanket, a dummy or soft toy. Children can also develop a comfort habit such as nail biting or thumb sucking. Almost all children use some form of comforter at times and the use of these does not indicate insecurity. Rather, they can promote security by helping a child to cope with separation from her mother, with anxiety or help her to feel calm and relaxed. Comforters only become a problem if they start to assume too great an importance in your child's life, or if they are accompanied by other signs of emotional upset or disturbance.

Most children grow out of using a comforter by the age of five, but some children may use them on their return from school or take them with them on an overnight stay, for several more years. Never stop your child from using a comforter, but if she spends all day clinging on to it or you feel she is too dependent on it, try to find out if anything is troubling her.

COMFORT OBJECTS

Your child may form a special attachment to a piece of blanket or a soft toy because she associates it with a pleasant or loving experience from the past. A cot blanket, for instance, may remind her of being wrapped up while her parents cuddle her, or a soft toy can be hugged close to help her fall asleep. If she is away from her home environment her comfort object can be a familiar reminder or link with this. Your child also may develop special rituals with her blanket such as sucking it, entwining it around her fingers or clutching it to her cheek. Some children may also

COMFORT COMES IN DIFFERENT SHAPES
Your child's comfort object – teddy, doll or blanket – brings her support and security.

FINGER SUCKING
Some children habitually suck their fingers for comfort and the more you remove them, the more they will persist in doing it.

use their comfort object as a safe way to get rid of some aggression – such as by biting or pulling at a toy's ears or legs.

Dummies Some babies like to suck more than others and dummies can be useful in helping to placate the sucking instinct or for soothing a fretful child. Dummies do not cause any damage to teeth in the first year unless coated with sweet or sugary substances, but can affect alignment if used long-term. Orthodontic dummies, therefore, should be used.

Most children discard dummies after the first year but it can be difficult for some toddlers to give up them up and many parents dislike seeing their child with a dummy once she is walking and talking. After the age of two or three it is reasonable to discourage your child from using a dummy. You can do this by gradually discarding it, by reducing the number of times a day she sucks the dummy, by 'losing' it, or by persuading your child to exchange it in return for a special treat. You could decide the 'giving up day' in advance so that your toddler is prepared.

COMFORT HABITS

Most young children develop certain habits that are carried out with little thought, but which worry or irritate their parents. Like a comfort object, some habits are used by children to help them feel more secure or release tension and often stop as the child gets older. Others, such as nail biting, sometimes persist into adult life.

Thumb and finger sucking Like dummies, thumb or finger sucking is a harmless habit in a young child. It usually starts in the second year.

Sucking can be a source of comfort to your child who may associate it with the pleasure of bottle or nipple sucking, closeness to you, and relief of hunger. Removing the thumb or fingers from the child's mouth or getting cross with her does not help.

If thumb sucking is ignored, most children grow out of the habit or it decreases by the age of four. After this age there is some concern from dental authorities that thumb sucking may displace the permanent teeth, but the sucking would have to be constant and extreme for this to happen.

A child may, however, be teased or thought babyish by others for sucking her thumb, and if it persists after the age of four it is best to try to divert her attention onto something else, or reward her for 'grown up' behaviour in stopping. Constant thumb sucking after this age may also indicate an emotional problem, and occasional thumb sucking may persist in some children at times of stress for many years.

Nail biting This is another common habit which usually occurs in children over the age of three. Often a child bites her nails without realising she is doing it, and as a way of relieving tension. Most children grow out of the habit, but in some children nail biting can become compulsive and persist into adolescence or adulthood. It is best to ignore occasional nail biting in a young child. Later on you can point out how ugly it looks and show your child how to take care of her nails like a 'grown up'.

Masturbation Most children occasionally handle their genitals for pleasure and it is a natural, perfectly normal activity which, for a toddler, has no sexual overtones. However, many parents feel uneasy or embarrassed when they see their child masturbating, especially if this is in public. The best way to deal with handling the genitals and masturbation is either to ignore it, or if you don't want your child to masturbate in front of you or others, either tell her so pleasantly or gently divert her hand and her attention to something else. Telling your child that it is naughty or wrong may make her feel guilty or she may grow up thinking her genitals are bad in some way and that adult sexual behaviour is nasty or furtive. If masturbation is frequent or excessive though, this may be a sign that your child is unhappy, or that there is some stress in her life. In this case, you will need to talk to your child to find out what is worrying her.

Head banging Some children bang their head in a rhythmical way before going to sleep at night, or during their sleep. This may be a soothing habit for them or a way of letting off steam and is rarely harmful. You could put extra padding in your child's cot or bed if necessary. Some children bang their heads on the floor during a tantrum but this is just to gain attention and most toddlers have the sense not to hurt themselves deliberately.

NICE NAILS
Young girls love wearing nail varnish and letting her paint her nails for fun may encourage her to be proud of them and stop biting them.

Hyperactivity

Also known as attention deficit disorder (ADD) or attention deficit hyperactivity disorder (ADHD), hyperactivity is a condition that has been recognised for many years. Its diagnosis and treatment is, however, often controversial. The term hyperactivity or ADD is usually used to describe young children who are thought to be overactive, impulsive, lack concentration or are difficult to manage. But most young children normally have high levels of activity and a child may be difficult to manage without being hyperactive. It can therefore be difficult for parents, and sometimes for health professionals, to decide whether a child is showing symptoms of hyperactivity, which requires early treatment and management, or whether he is just displaying 'normal' behaviour problems. There are also varying degrees of hyperactivity and some children may suffer from a mild form, while other children may be more severely affected.

Active or hyperactive children?

It is essential not to label a child who just shows normal childhood behaviour as hyperactive. Your child is unlikely to be suffering from hyper-activity, for example, if he is just exuberant or full of energy and is sometimes disobedient, defiant or naughty. Further, your toddler is not hyperactive just because he gets fidgety while you are having a long conversation with another adult, refuses to sit still for long, such as when at the table, or is restless on a long journey.

Most children get aggressive or have temper tantrums occasionally, as well as getting active when it is time for bed or in a new place such as a supermarket. Boredom is guaranteed to make the most placid child act up in some way, which is not necessarily a sign of hyperactivity.

A noisy or uninhibited child is not the same as a hyperactive one, nor is one that wakes up full of energy at six in the morning.

Finally, a child who is having behaviour problems because he is suffering from stress for any reason should not be labelled hyperactive.

Features of hyperactivity

While it is difficult to tell the difference between the above 'normal' behaviour patterns and

Unpredictable
Hyperactive toddlers may behave erratically, enjoying looking at something one minute and destroying it the next.

hyperactive behaviour, there are some distinctive differences. A hyperactive child is more likely to have had many of the following symptoms as a baby: screamed or cried constantly, needed very little sleep or had irregular sleep patterns, was difficult to settle and woke up constantly, had colic and was difficult to feed, was irritable and disliked being cuddled, jumped at every sound, had excessive dribbling and was very thirsty, head banged or cot rocked persistently.

Much of the following behaviour is also fairly typical for two-year-olds. But an older toddler who has had many of the symptoms below for at least six months, may be hyperactive:

★ Is clumsy or accident prone.
★ Constantly fidgets and dislikes staying still or sitting even for short periods.
★ Is frequently aggressive.
★ Flits from one thing to another, lacks concentration and never finishes what he is doing.
★ Overreacts to minor things and is difficult to calm down.
★ Has continual sleep problems.
★ Has difficulty in learning to dress himself.
★ Has poor self-esteem.
★ Has difficulty in taking turns.
★ Touches and meddles with everything.
★ Has speech delay or talks continually.
★ Has a poor appetite and is always thirsty.

★ Does dangerous things without any sense of danger or sign of fear.
★ Dislikes change.
★ Has health problems such as ear or chest infections, asthma, eczema and tummy aches.

CAUSES OF HYPERACTIVITY

There are many theories about what triggers hyperactivity but no clear cause has been found.

Genetic As most hyperactive children have at least one close relative who was hyperactive as a child, it is thought that hyperactivity may have an hereditary component. However, no specific gene has yet been identified. Hyperactivity is much more common in boys than girls (about five boys to every girl) and a large percentage of hyperactive boys are blonde and blue-eyed.

Maternal health A high proportion of hyperactive children are born into families where there is a history of allergy in the mother, such as hayfever, asthma, eczema or migraine.

Pregnancy and birth Problems in pregnancy such as allergy and stress, and birth complications may contribute to hyperactivity.

Environmental factors Adverse conditions such as lead and nitrates in tap water, exhaust fumes, pesticides and other chemicals may be responsible.

Essential fatty acid deficiency Studies in the UK and the USA have found that some hyperactive children are deficient in essential fatty acids. Symptoms of essential fatty acid deficiency include severe thirst, dry skin and hair, frequent urination, and a history of allergies such as asthma and eczema.

Nutritional deficiencies Some hyperactive children may be low in zinc, magnesium or vitamin B12.

Foods Additives, colourings, preservatives, chocolate, sugar, dairy products, wheat, tomatoes, nitrates, oranges, eggs and other foods, have been implicated as a possible cause of hyperactivity.

TREATMENT OF HYPERACTIVITY

If your child has many of the symptoms of hyperactivity you need to work out ways of dealing with it. A hyperactive child needs to be treated firmly but not harshly – constant punishment will make him worse. He also needs a stable routine and as much love as any other child, even though you may feel very unloving as he destroys the house! Making the house as childproof as possible is a must (see page 50).

If cannot cope with your child's behaviour, consult your health visitor or doctor for a specialist assessment. If hyperactivity is diagnosed, treatment may include behavioural modification therapy, medication such as Ritalin or dietary intervention. You may also be able to get help from a Hyperactive or ADD support group.

Diets and hyperactivity Whether eating certain foods leads to hyperactivity is not proved but your child will not come to any harm if you cut out processed foods and drinks containing additives, colourings or preservatives or, if you suspect these affect his behaviour, foods such as tomatoes or excess sugar. It can be dangerous, however, to substitute or exclude some foods from your child's diet: for instance, soy milk can also cause allergies if substituted for cow's milk while a lack of foods such as dairy products or wheat may cause nutritional deficiencies.

If you suspect that your child's behaviour is affected by such foods, then you should seek advice from your health visitor or a dietitian (see page 11).

UNSOCIAL BEHAVIOUR
A hyperactive child often behaves in a very disruptive manner, having frequent temper tantrums, throwing things around and refusing to sit still and do what he is told.

JEALOUSY AND RIVALRY

Jealousy is a common and natural emotion in children and may first show itself in toddlers when a new baby arrives in the family. This is known as sibling rivalry. Until that time, a first born toddler has had her parents all to herself, and has not had to compete with anyone else for their love or attention.

With the birth of a sibling, a child is now bound to experience less of her mother's time and attention and may fear that she is no longer loved or cared about by her parents. In addition, a new baby means there is bound to be some disruption in a toddler's daily routine, with perhaps the temporary loss of walks or little treats, and she may resent the change in her special relationship with her parents.

It is also common for children to be jealous if they think that their parents love another sibling more than them.

Given the amount of adjustment a toddler has to make when a new baby arrives in the family, it is not surprising that even if she feels pleasure and affection for the baby, her strongest reactions may be jealousy and resentment, at least some of the time. This may have several effects:

★ **Regression to an earlier stage of behaviour** A toddler who is dry and clean by day may start wetting or soiling herself again, want to wear a nappy or she may want to drink from a bottle instead of a cup.

★ **Anti-social behaviour** A toddler may hit other children or her parents, or try to hurt the baby.

★ **Attention-seeking behaviour** A toddler may be deliberately naughty when her mother is attending to the baby. She may want her mother to play with her, cuddle her, or take her to the toilet.

★ **Being defiant** Your previously compliant toddler may become disobedient at every opportunity.

★ **Being weepy** A jealous toddler is an insecure one and may become clingy or withdrawn.

★ **Rejection** A toddler may reject her mother to get back at her and transfer her affections to her father or another adult, often a close relative such as a grandmother.

HELPING YOUR TODDLER COPE

Although some problems are bound to occur occasionally, with proper measures and handling, these can be kept to a minimum and the amount of jealousy reduced.

Prepare her for the new baby How soon you tell your toddler about a new baby will depend to some extent on her age and understanding. Nine months is a long time to a small child who may think the baby is never going to appear. But don't wait until the last minute to spring the idea of a new baby on your child. Introduce the idea when you feel the time is right for her and over the following months talk to her about the new baby in a realistic way. Explain that the baby will be

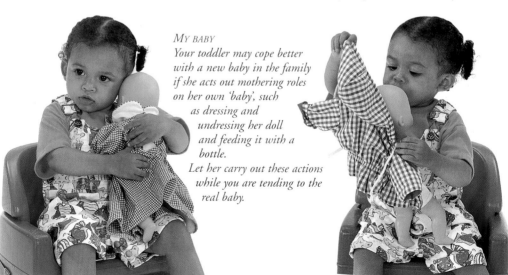

MY BABY
Your toddler may cope better with a new baby in the family if she acts out mothering roles on her own 'baby', such as dressing and undressing her doll and feeding it with a bottle.
Let her carry out these actions while you are tending to the real baby.

too small for her to play with at first and that he may cry a lot to begin with and will need feeding and your attention. As your abdomen expands, let your child feel the baby moving and growing.

Going into hospital If she is old enough to understand, explain that you will be going into hospital to have the baby (if that is the case), and who will be looking after her while you are away. Leave your child with someone she knows well.

Meeting the baby Let your child visit you in hospital and have a present ready for her 'from the baby'. Try not to be cuddling your baby when your toddler is first introduced to him. Ask visitors to make a fuss of your toddler before noticing the baby and to ask her what the baby's name is or to show them the baby.

When visitors comment on how cute or pretty the new baby is, make similar comments about your toddler, such as 'he's cute just like his sister'.

Give her extra time and attention Try not to let your baby monopolise all your time. Give your toddler extra cuddles and reassure her that you still love her. Try to make a special time for her when the baby is asleep or if possible leave the baby with someone else sometimes and take your toddler out somewhere alone.

Involve her with the baby Ask her to 'help' you look after the baby – she could fetch a clean nappy or get baby's clothes out of the drawer. You could also encourage her to sing to the baby.

Expect her to be angry or regress to babyish behaviour Go along with babyish behaviour if she needs this but also stress how clever she is and how much more she can do compared to the baby, such as opening doors, playing with various toys, dressing herself and so on.

If she is old enough, talk to her about her feelings and acknowledge that she may get fed up at times with the baby crying, or always needing feeding. Tell her that she too used to be a baby and her little sibling will grow big just like her.

Maintain routine It is important to avoid introducing any further big changes into your toddler's life. It is better to delay starting your child at playgroup or beginning potty training until things settle down a bit, or to do these well in advance of the baby being born.

Aggression towards the baby Sometimes a loving pat can become aggressive or your toddler may poke or deliberately attack the baby. Make it clear that she must not hurt the baby, but guard against

SIBLING LOVE
Involve your toddler with your baby as much as possible. Encourage him to touch the baby and take an interest in what you are doing with the baby.

being over protective or scolding if your toddler approaches the baby.

If you feel your toddler will hurt your baby, don't leave them alone together but involve her under supervision. Let her hold the baby while you maintain a secure hold too. Encourage her to sing and talk to him and to try to get the baby to smile at her. When the baby responds, point out that he likes her.

Be prepared for a delayed reaction Even if your toddler seems happy with the baby at first, she may not have realised that the baby is here to stay and will continue to demand your attention. So don't be surprised if a few weeks or months later she starts to play up, or suddenly refuses to go to playgroup. Again be patient and understanding about this and stress the advantages of what she can do, compared to the baby. Also remind her that in no time at all her new sibling will be big enough to play with her.

SPOILING AND MANNERS

Every child needs to be spoiled or indulged once in a while and to have her reasonable needs for your love, time and attention met. These make a child feel loved and secure. But when a child is given too many possessions or anything she asks for, is constantly the centre of attention, is seldom or never disciplined, and her needs are always paramount to those of her parents or other people, she will grow up expecting the world to revolve around her all the time and becomes a very demanding child.

Getting the balance right between loving and overindulging a child can sometimes be difficult and there are some situations where it is easy to spoil or overindulge her: for example, if the child is ill, especially if the illness is frequent; if the mother goes out to work and feels guilty about not being there for her child; if the father is away from home a lot or the parents are separated; or if one parent is too strict, the other parent may want to compensate by being overindulgent.

Spoiling is also common if the child is an only or much longed for child or if she is the first or only grandchild. Grandparents may overindulge the child and override the parents' wishes.

Parents who have had a deprived childhood themselves may wish to give their child what they never had. If the child's friends have lots of things and the parents don't want their child to miss out they may also spoil her.

It's all very well to have good intentions towards your child, but spoiling her may lead to behavioural problems now and social problems as she gets older. A spoilt or overindulged child who is given everything she wants and who has no limits set on her behaviour is likely to be:

★ Unpopular with other children because she always wants her own way.
★ Insecure because no limits have been set on the way she behaves.
★ Greedy because she expects to get more than others.
★ Selfish because she has never been taught to share.
★ Disobedient because she has always been allowed to do what she wants.
★ Inconsiderate of other people's feelings.
★ Impossible to satisfy.

GIVE ME!
Until your toddler learns the concept of sharing and consideration for others she will continue to think that grabbing is the best way to get what she wants. It may seem like a fun game now but she needs to learn that it is socially unacceptable.

★ Constantly whinging, whining or moaning.
★ Rude and bad mannered.

COURTESY COUNTS

Being courteous and well mannered are social skills that do not come automatically to young children – they must be learned. Knowing what may be acceptable in one situation, but rude in another, can be very confusing for them. For example, why can she ask for a drink at home if she's thirsty, but not at someone else's house? Or why can daddy make a remark about a neighbour, but she is told she's being rude when she repeats it? Learning how to behave appropriately is an important part of your child's social development. Children who have been taught to behave in a well-mannered way will feel socially confident in different kinds of situations and company, are usually viewed positively by other people and tend to be more popular. They are less likely to cause embarrassment to their parents, are considerate of other people's feelings and are more likely to have respect and empathy for others.

GOOD MANNERS

If you want your child to grow up with good manners, it is important to set a good example yourself. If you interrupt your child when she is talking to you, forget to say please or thank you, push in front of a queue or make rude comments about other people, then your child is likely to copy you. But as well as learning by copying you, you can also help your child to learn good manners in several ways.

Teach her to say 'please' and 'thank you' from an early age. As soon as she is old enough to understand, explain to her why it is important to be considerate to other people, wait turns and share things. Although she will not grasp all this immediately, you are laying the foundation for good manners for the future.

Anticipate situations where she may forget to say hello, or please or thank you, and remind her beforehand. For example, 'can you remember to say thank you to John's mummy after you have had tea there this afternoon'.

When she shows good manners, let her know that you noticed and are pleased with her. Similarly, when she has deliberately and knowingly behaved badly towards someone, tell her it is unacceptable.

WOULD YOU LIKE SOME?
From about the age of three, children can learn to share food and pass it to others. They will also learn to eat less messily and not to grab food.

CORRECTING BAD MANNERS

Good manners are not learnt overnight but progressively over the years as your child grows and learns. It is important not to put too much pressure on your child to be well mannered too soon, to the extent that she becomes inhibited and anxious about always doing everything right. Most young children are rude or bad mannered at times, for instance if they are angry or want to show off. In these cases, depending on the cause, you may choose to ignore her behaviour, acknowledge how she is feeling or let her know what the limits are.

Sometimes too, bad manners may simply be a matter of forgetting or of excitement. For instance, she may be excited about trying out a new piece of equipment in the park and rush to the front of the queue without thinking. Here, a gentle reminder that others were waiting before her is all that is necessary. Be aware too of when she is too shy or embarrassed to say please or thank you to someone, and don't make an issue of it. Instead, say them for her – by hearing you she will eventually learn to say them for herself.

DISCIPLINE AND PUNISHMENT

Children need boundaries regarding their behaviour. Knowing what's expected of them and how far they can go makes them feel safe and secure. Toddlerhood is a time when guidelines and controls over bad behaviour need to be introduced and limits set. But it is also a time when a young child is only just starting to learn how to control her body and her behaviour. So any discipline and punishment should be appropriate to your child's age and understanding.

Even when your child is old enough to understand the rules and know the limits, it is normal if she tries to push them, just to see how far you will let her go.

Often you can head off potential conflict by anticipating misbehaviour and removing your child from the scene, being aware of trigger factors, ignoring minor offences and not saying 'no' all the time.

RULES FOR DISCIPLINE

It is most important that you are consistent. Set reasonable limits and stick to them. Your child will get very confused and frustrated if she is allowed to do something one day and gets into trouble for it the next. Similarly, both parents should agree on discipline and avoid giving your child the chance to manipulate one parent against the other by bending the rules. Make sure you explain your rules to your toddler in a way that she can understand. Explain the reasons for the rules, for instance why she should put her toys away: so that nobody trips over them and gets hurt.

Give clear guidelines about rules and be specific when you want your child to do something, rather than make vague statements. Likewise, explain why you are punishing her, for instance because she hit someone again after she was told off the first time. Don't punish twice. If your child has already been punished by one parent she should not be punished again by the other.

Praise your child when she has behaved well, rather than only commenting on negative behaviour. Positive reinforcement is usually more effective in the long-term.

Don't make empty threats. Only threaten punishments if you are going to carry them out otherwise it won't take long for your toddler to call your bluff.

Do make it up afterwards. Once your child has been punished, let her know you still love her, and move on to other things.

Before you punish your child for misbehaviour give her a chance to try alternative behaviour, or time to respond to your request. For example, suggest 'why don't you go and kick your ball in the garden instead of kicking the table?' If she ignores you, warn her of the consequences, such as 'time out' (see page 95). Or if she refuses to pick up her toys tell her calmly 'you have until the count of ten to start picking up your toys'. Start counting and if she has not complied with your request by the time you reach ten, back it up with 'time out' immediately. Don't discuss the issue or offer to count to ten again.

METHODS OF PUNISHMENT

Reprimand This is the most common method of correcting behaviour. Children want to please their parents and a stern 'telling off' when your child is doing or has done something wrong can be effective. But it will only work if it is used sparingly and with conviction. Constantly telling your child off for the slightest thing will have a negative effect, and she will cease to listen. When telling your child off:

SET AN EXAMPLE
It is important that you practise your own rules – if you are always telling your child she cannot eat sweets before dinner then don't do it in front of her yourself.

- ★ Make sure you have her full attention – look her in the face by bending down to her level or sitting her up on a chair or table.
- ★ Make your voice firm and confident, keep your words short and to the point, but make it clear why you are cross.
- ★ Point out the consequences of what will happen if she continues the behaviour.
- ★ Check that she has understood what you have said.

Smacking Most parents are tempted to smack their child at times, and many feel a short smack is an effective way of dealing with bad behaviour but smacking should never be the main form of discipline. If you do smack, it should be done immediately and sparingly, such as a short tap on the hand when your child is heading into danger and other tactics have failed. Only your hands should be used and only one smack should be given. It should only ever be used as a last resort if at all.

Smacking is forbidden in several countries. Even if it is not illegal, there are several reasons why smacking children is best avoided:

It can be dangerous. Smacking is usually done when a parent is angry and you can cause injury if you accidentally hit your child too hard. Or if a short tap does not work, it can get out of control with the parent hitting harder next time to get the message across.

Smacking is usually ineffective. Research has found that the more a child is smacked, the less notice she takes. Or a child does not know or understand why she was smacked.

It can induce aggressive behaviour in a child. Aggression breeds aggression. Your child may think that if it is all right for you to smack, then she can do so too.

Time out This is a simple, unemotional and effective way of correcting behaviour or removing your child from a deteriorating situation. When she misbehaves, remove her from the area to a separate room and tell her to sit quietly on a chair. Tell her why she's having time out. The room should be safe and preferably unstimulating such as a hall, and the chair small enough for her to climb on herself. The time need not be for very

ACT APPROPRIATELY
Punishment should only be given when your child has misbehaved in spite of being told not to do something. If, however, he does not know that pulling a tape out means it doesn't work any more, then a simple reprimand should suffice.

long – around a minute for each year of your child's age – a timer is useful. If she comes out of the room before you tell her to, calmly put her back again and hold her on the chair if necessary until the time is up. If the chair has to be in the same room as you, do not allow any talking. Once her time is up, give her a cuddle and forget the incident. Don't use time out for every little incidence or a toddler could be on the chair all day.

BE FIRM
Unless you sound firm your toddler may just think that reprimands such as 'pick up your clothes' are the signal for a game to begin.

INDEX

ACKNOWLEDGEMENTS

Carroll & Brown would very
much like to thank:

Rachel Attfield, Kim Menzies
and Bettina Graham for hair
and make-up

Simon Wright for
photographic assistance

Sally Powell for additional
design

Maddalena Bastianelli for
props assistance

Joanne Stanford for the index

Sandra Schneider for picture
research

Dorian Cassidy for
administrative assistance

Children's World for the use of
their clothes

Debenham's for the use of their
clothes

Picture credits:
page 47: top – Scott
Camazine/Oxford Scientific
Films; middle – Dr H.C.
Robinson/SPL; bottom – Dr P.
Marazzi/SPL; page 48: Dr
Pollock/St Mary's Hospital
Medical School; page 49: top
and bottom left – Dr P.
Marazzi/SPL; right – SPL

Publishing director
Denis Kennedy

Art director
Chrissie Lloyd

Editor
Sharon Freed

Assistant editor
Nadia Silver

Art editor
Mercedes Morgan

Designers
Karen Sawyer, Adelle Morris

Photography
Mike Good

Illustrator
Conny Jude

Production
Christine Corton,
Wendy Rogers